MW00781805

COMING CLEAN

To my Sister Pliina
Thanks for your support
Jessie 3/18/23

JESSIE WARREN

Copyright © 2021 Jessie Warren
All rights reserved
First Edition

Fulton Books, Inc.
Meadville, PA

Published by Fulton Books 2021

ISBN 978-1-63710-700-3 (paperback)
ISBN 978-1-63710-701-0 (digital)

Printed in the United States of America

This book is dedicated to my five daughters,
Chantel, Wynette, Vernell, Cassandra, and Veronica.
Also in loving memory of my heart Joan.

Mama

Mama was an alcoholic for most of her life. She suffered many of the hardships that being an alcoholic brought. From a child to becoming an adult, I fought the bottle with her. She would scratch blood from my arms as I poured her liquor down the drain. That did not work. I furnished her entire apartment after she promised me she would not drink anymore. She could not keep her promise. I remember threatening bootleggers that I would burn down their houses if they sold her anything to drink. I even threatened liquor store owners, but that did not work. My mama died February 28, 1993, but by the grace and mercy of God, she had lived clean of alcohol the last fourteen years of her life, and I will write about those fourteen years.

Mama moved to Virginia to settle my stepfather's estate. He had left some property, and since they never divorced, she had the power of attorney. In New York, I got the word that Mama had stopped drinking. I did not believe it after all that she had been through and all the failed attempts to stop in the past. I had given up hope that she would stop. But I am glad God did not give up on my mama. God's blessings extend from everlasting to everlasting. He blessed me to spend six years with my mama before he took her up in glory. I will cherish those years and will be forever thankful. During those years, my mama and I got the opportunity to mend some fences. I was well aware of the resentment I had against my father for they were many, and they were deep, but I was not as aware that I had some even deeper resentments that I held against my mother.

I had been in Virginia for about a year. I was at work one day when I received word that my mama had suffered a stroke and was rushed to the hospital. When I walked into her room. She was lying in bed sleeping after being sedated by the doctors. I noticed she had a needle in her hand with nothing connected to it. I asked the doctor why it was there, and he told me because oftentimes stroke victims would suffer additional strokes, and if that happened, they would not have to search for a vein. It was at that moment I realized my mama was mortal. You sorta think your parents will live forever. I remember Mama telling me, "You all are going to miss me when I am gone," and I would say, "You are not going anywhere. You will live to see your great-great-great-grandchildren." Now I sit looking at the face of my frail mama and thinking I could lose her.

Mama recovered from the stroke and came home, but that thought of her mortality stayed with me. I never told her about it, but it brought me closer to her. It motivated me to get to know my mama on a much deeper level. I would call her and tell her I was on my way over and if there was anything she needed. Usually, she would say, "Bring me a soda," and I would pick up a case. I had begun to spend time with her. I would stop over, and sometimes, Mama would be getting ready to soak her feet in a foot tub. I would take the tub fill it full of hot water and get a bar of ivory soap along with a sponge and a towel. I would soap the sponge really good and soak her feet for a few minutes in the hot water. Then I would take one foot at a time and wash it. I would put so much soap on her feet from the sponge that her feet would be nice and soapy. Then I would work the soap between each toe and massage her foot from toe to heel. I would tease her with this little piggy went to market, and she would laugh. More important than pampering her was the talking we did. I remember asking her, during one of her foot massages, "Mama, have you ever been in love?" She answered off the top of her head and said, "Yes, of course." I said again, "Mama, tell me if you have ever been in love." This time, she thought about it, sadly shook her head, and said no.

Here, my mama is in her sixties and has never been in love. I took it upon myself to show her love and to show her what love is. I started by telling her how much I loved her, and I began hugging her. When I hugged her, she did not return the hug. She kept her arms down by her side, but I was determined and did not allow that to stop me. I continued to be affectionate with her. And one day, I went to hug her, and lo and behold, she hugged me back. I knew I was getting through that wall she had erected over the years. I understood that because she had so many children, she did not have time for love.

Life has a way of revisiting us through regrets, resentments, things we should have done, and things we did. Mama was no different. In her final years, her life revisited her, and she had a lot of regrets especially when it came to her children. Mama never told me this, but as I watched her dealing with her sobriety, she would go out of her way for us even though we were grown. When I called her from New York and told her I wanted to come to Virginia with my family, even though she had only three bedrooms, and I had a wife and three children, she saw it as a chance to make up for some of the things she did not do for me as a boy, and she said without any hesitation, "Come on." Mama would give up her last dime if one of her children asked for it. I remember how important her life insurance was to her, but there were times she would give my brother her insurance premium to pay his rent and then come to me for the money to pay her insurance. She just wanted to make up for her past, and I understood that.

Mama was brought up in the church, and through God's great mercy and grace, she found her way back. She rejoined the choir. I was brought up in the church also, and that same mercy and grace were extended to me. I found my way back, but during this time, I was still on the outside and would only attend church on those occasions when my mother had a special program or Easter. On those occasions, I would sit in the pews and look at my Mama singing, and I could see her journey. I knew how far she had come to get back.

One night, my mama called and told me she was experiencing some pain in her chest. She wanted to go to the hospital, so I got dressed and went to see about her. When I got there, Mama was dressed and ready. She tried to put on a strong front, but I knew there was something wrong because she never would have called me at this time of the night if she was not in pain. I drove her to the emergency room, and after the usual three-hour wait, the nurse called her name, and we went back to the examination room. When the doctor came in, Mama told him she was having pains in her chest, and he asked her to undress. I left the room and went to my car for a smoke and after a while went back in. They had taken her for x-rays, and she was sitting on the table. Mama told me that she overheard the doctors talking, and one spelled out the word tumor to the other doctor. She had this worried look on her face.

I told her, "They were probably talking about some other patient, and you are just being nosy as usual and thinking they were talking about you."

The doctor gave her a prescription for the pain and told her to make an appointment with her private doctor and that the hospital would send her x-ray to him. As we drove home, I could tell Mama was worried, and as for me, I kept thinking about that word the doctor spelled out—tumor. The thoughts of her mortality returned.

Mama made an appointment with her doctor immediately and asked me to go with her.

I said, "Of course, I will go."

When we arrived at the doctor's office, he had already received and looked at the x-rays. My mama and I sat down. The doctor confirmed what the emergency room doctor spelled out. He confirmed that there was a spot on her lung, and it looked like cancer. He said he would have to take further tests to be sure and that he would have to take a biopsy to be 100 percent sure. I remember thinking, *I wish you would have waited until you were 100 percent before you use the word cancer.* I could tell Mama was scared, but she attempted to be brave. I think a lot of her fear was that she was not going to have enough time to make up for the things she did not do. As we drove home from the doctor's office, Mama told me that before we know for sure to keep this between us. I told her I would, and I tried to encourage her and tell her that everything would be all right. No matter what, we would beat it.

Once the news was confirmed that it was lung cancer, we were already getting close, but the news brought us even closer. I began spending every spare moment with her. When she called, I would go see her. The doctor started her on chemo. I was there holding her hand at every session. Eventually, she was hospitalized as the cancer continued to spread. My mama and I talked about everything at the end including the forgiveness of her children. She wanted us to forgive her for not being the perfect mother. She asked if I could forgive her, and I, in turn, asked if she could forgive me. Mama told me that she was not afraid of death because God had allowed her to live to see her children grow, her grandchildren, and she had even been blessed to see a great-grandchild born. She said she did not want to suffer and asked me to promise her that when the time came to not allow them to hook her up to a machine or do anything to bring her back. I believe she told me this because she knew I would carry out her wishes. We would pray together for God to take her home even though I wanted my mother to live, but that would have been selfish on my part, so I joined her in prayer.

During the last years, the relationship between my mama and me transcended different levels. We went through a level of resentments, guilt, shame, and regrets to through forgiveness and love, and at the end, we became friends. I saw my mama as a human being and, under the circumstances, doing the best she could with what she had. I told the doctors, in order to follow her wishes, that when the time came to make her comfortable. On February 28, 1993, my mama died. I am so thankful to God that she knew love and that I was a part of it.

I Don't Remember Being a Child

—⟡—

I was ten or twelve years old when I got caught smoking by my stepfather. He was drunk and angry. And he decided to break me out of smoking by beating me. He tied me up and said he would teach me not to smoke. He would often get drunk and beat me. He stayed angry with my mother, and the only way he could get back at her was to beat me. While he was tying me up, I made up my mind that I was not going to cry. I was not going to give him the satisfaction of seeing me cry.

He took the electric cord, doubled it into a loop, and began to hit me saying, "I will teach you not to smoke." The more he hit me, the more determined I was not to shed a tear. It occurred to him that I was not hollering and crying, and he stated, "You are a man now, huh, and you are not going to cry?" Then he started to really lay it on. He was determined to make me cry, and I was just as determined not to, and I did not. I just stood there, staring at him, as he hit me. I began to bite my bottom lip. I bit my lip so hard I could taste blood.

He beat me so bad that day that the electric cord tore through my shirt and skin. I am fifty-six years old now, and I still carry the scars on my back and stomach from that beating. But I never shed a tear. He then put me into a dark closet and shut the door. As I lay in that dark musky closet, I refused to cry. I think I had run out of tears. My need to cry turned into anger and hate, and I made up my mind that night that I was going to kill this man for what he did.

After that beating, my stepfather never hit me again. I had discovered that I had a power to use against abusive adults that would come into my life, from my stepfather to the bullies to the attendant at the reform school, and that power consisted of not crying no matter what. I did not just limit my newly discovered power against abusive adults, but I used against life itself. No matter how much pain or hurt would come my way, I was not going to give anyone or anything the satisfaction of seeing Ronnie cry. I am a man now. I am twelve years old, and I am a man now.

At forty-six, life had beaten me down, and I started having thoughts of killing myself. One day, I was walking by a chapel, and I went in. The chapel was empty, and I walked up to the front pew and took a seat. Up to this point, I had prayed, but I had never done this aloud. I always prayed in my head, in my mind. I never cried out, not even to God, and all of a sudden, I had an overwhelming urge to cry out to God and to verbalize what was going on with me. I opened my mouth and began to tell God all about it. I walked up to the altar of that chapel, fell on my knees, and cried out to God. The tears came as I told God about that beating I took, not just that beating but all the beatings. As I told God about all the abuse, I could feel God's arms wrap around me and his sweet voice saying, "I know. I know. Let it out." I cried and cried and thought I would never stop crying. But God sat with me and listened and comforted me.

In life, things happen to us, people hurt us, we have hurt people, and we have choked back the tears. Because we did not shed the tears, we believed that we got over the pains. But those tears did not go away. They were just held back, choked back. They have been put in a bottle within our hearts and corked never to be let out. Then God comes along, uncorks the bottle, and allows us to cry it all out.

Some of us have tears from forty to fifty years ago that were never cried when they were supposed to be. Now in the arms of God, you can let it go and cry. You can go ahead and free yourself.

I have spent a large part of my life running away from myself. I was born to an impoverished family and a life consisting of hunger, abuse, and neglect. My father left the day I was born and never returned. Questions about the fairness of life started early for me. I began asking, why me?

I have been freed to write this book because the people I would hurt the most have passed on, and those that are still living, well, maybe it will serve to bring them closer to the light. That is my prayer.

I was having a conversation with my sister one day, and she said something that rang so true.

She said, "Ronnie, I don't remember you ever being a child. It seems to me you have been grown ever since I can remember."

I was so touched by her statement, especially since I was only a year older than her. Then about two months later, I was having a conversation with a friend that my sister and I grew up with, and she said to me, "Ronnie, you know I do not remember you ever being a child. It seems to me you have been grown ever since I have known you."

Again, I was moved because I was only a year ahead of her as well. When I thought about it, I do not remember being a child either. But I must have been a child. It just seems, with no adult to be responsible, I was forced to think adult thoughts and make adult decisions. You may call this a coincidence, but today, I do not believe in coincidences anymore. I've lived long enough to see it is all planned. I have often said I was robbed of my childhood and to have these two women who knew me during that time child, to come to me and say I was never a child, that to them I was grown ever since they knew me despite the fact I was only one year older.

I did not have time to be a child due to the circumstances to which I was born. Both of the adults in the house were alcoholics. I was one of eight children. You may think I was the oldest, but I was not. I had a brother and a sister that were older than me. My older brother ran away early, he could not take it, and my older sister was retarded. This left me with two choices run away or stay to look out for my younger sisters and brothers. Running away was never an option for me. I never thought to run but to stay and help.

As I said, my mama and stepfather in the house were alcoholics. They would start drinking on Friday, and it would last throughout the entire weekend and sometimes into the following week. During these drinking binges (don't ask me how), they would forget they had eight children in the house. Since they were not there, my siblings looked to me for their needs since I was the oldest, and I felt it was my responsibility to take care of them.

There were many mornings when one of my siblings, usually my baby brother, would wake me up crying because he was hungry. I would wake, and there they all stood crying in unison, "Ronnie, Ronnie, we hungry." I would get up and go to the kitchen, and they would follow. More times than not, there would be no food, which meant the drinking had started before my parents bought groceries. How could two adults forget to buy food? I did not understand, but I did not have time to spend figuring this out because here were my siblings sitting around the table looking at me. They would stop crying because they believed I would give them something to eat, and I did. I was only eight years old, but I was all they had.

As I have said, there were a lot of times when there was no food in the house, but I had to find something for them to eat. I remember one occasion when I opened the cabinet, and there was a bag of cornmeal. I remembered watching my mother cook corn bread cakes atop the stove in a frying pan. It looked easy to do, so I took out the cornmeal and looked for milk in the refrigerator, and there was none. No problem, I will use water. Then I looked for some grease. I remembered my mother using grease, but there was none. Now I had a problem. I looked at my siblings, and they sat there looking at me. I had to do something. Then I got an idea (please keep in mind I was only eight years old at the time). I got out a can of hair grease called My Knight. I mixed up the meal with water, put the hair grease in the frying pan, and fried the bread. It worked. The bread turned brown. My siblings stood in line with their plates in hand as I placed the bread on their plates. Yes, I had my plate too. We all sat down to eat.

It had become a habit for my parents to leave on their drinking sprees and leaving me to take care of the kids, never thinking that I was a kid myself. One morning, I woke up, and there was nothing to eat, not even cornmeal. I knew I had to do something. I told the kids to stay in the house, and I would go find Mama and bring back some food.

I went to a couple of houses that sold alcohol which I knew my mother frequented, but she was not at any of them. My sisters' and brothers' faces came to me, and I thought I have got to do something. As I walked the street looking for my mama (I never looked for my stepfather), she was nowhere to be found. I walked past the schoolyard where White kids went to school and remember watching the White kids play. They laughed and played as if they did not have a care in the world, and here I was with the responsibility of six children at the age of eight. The bell rang, and the White kids lined up to go inside. I wished I could have gotten in line to go inside. But I had to stop dreaming and come up with something for my siblings to eat.

I walked along the fence of the schoolyard when I noticed the janitor emptying trash cans into a large dumpster. After he emptied the last can, he went back inside the school. Looking around and making sure no one saw me, I made my way toward the dumpster. I peeked inside and saw a lot of sandwich bags. I picked up one and found a discarded peanut butter and jelly sandwich. I picked up another bag and found a ham sandwich. I could not believe my eyes, and I thought these kids must have it good if they can afford to throw away whole sandwiches. I took all the sandwiches I could carry in a large bag I found.

When I returned home, my sisters and brothers were disappointed because Mama was not with me, but their disappointment vanished when they saw the sandwiches. We sat and ate until we were full, and we still had some sandwiches left. There were a lot of kids in my neighborhood that were neglected, so I gave them the sandwiches I had left over. It is for this reason that the woman said she could not recall me being a child. She was one of the neglected kids in the neighborhood.

My house was full of abuse, every type and on all levels. The abuse affected all of the members of the household, but it was targeted at me mostly. My stepfather would beat my mother after or during an argument, and I would come to her defense. I was never a child in the sense of being a child. By coming to my mother's defense,

I would suffer the wrath of my stepfather. He abused me for many reasons, however the main one was he wasn't my father. He had four sons by my mother, which were my younger brothers. He treated his sons better than he treated my sister and me. The other reason he abused me was he felt he could get back at my mother by hurting me. He could not hurt my mother enough. My mother was a very attractive woman and loved to party and often went out alone, and this angered him. I remember my mother would leave before he got home from work, and I knew that when he got home, and she was gone, he would start on me. I would plead with my mama as she dressed, begging her not to go or to take me and my sister with her. The more I pleaded, the more she would try to convince me that he was not going to do anything to me or my sisters. She advised me to "just don't say anything" and stay out of his way, and he would not bother us. I knew different, but there was nothing I could do to convince her not to go out or to take me with her.

My mother did not believe it was as bad as I said it was, so she would leave me there and go out to party. My stepfather would come home and find her gone and start out calling her bitch, whore, slut, and everything else he could think of. Then he would turn his anger at me. He would look in my direction and begin calling me names. He would start with bastard, asking why she didn't take this bigheaded bastard with her. After ranting and raving for a while, he would leave, and I knew when he returned, the physical abuse would start. During one such time, I was shoved down a flight of stairs after he got drunk. I was in his way when he was trying to go down the steps, so he shoved me. The fall resulted in my leg being broken in three places below the knee. I have some bruises on my body from him that I will take to my grave. Eventually I got to the point that when my mother left the house by the front door, I would take my sister and go out the back door.

My sister and I would roam the streets for the entire week-end sometimes and would not return home until we were sure our mother had returned. I can remember sneaking around the outside of the house, listening for her voice or any sign that she was home. If we did not get any sign, it was back to the streets. I look back now and wonder how we made it. We slept in cars or car lots, hallways, back porches, and even under houses. Strangers would see us, take us home, and feed us, sometimes giving us some clothes.

One night, it had started to rain, and we were so tired. My sister and I sat down on the curb. She began to cry, and I remember putting my arm around her to console her. I looked up as the rain hit my face, and I began to cry, but because it was raining, my sister could not see my tears. I could not allow her to see me cry. I had to be strong for her sake.

The abuse of my stepfather continued, but never mind that. It was my absence from school that got the attention of the Department of Social Services. Once they began to investigate my homelife, they decided to take me out of the house and placed me into the foster care system. I did not want to go into foster care. I wanted to stay with my mother and take care of her and my siblings. But I had no choice in the matter. The Department of Social Services finished their investigation, and their decision was final.

The first family I was placed with lived not far from my house. In the beginning, I would leave the house a little early for school so I could stop by and see my sister and brothers while they were getting ready for school. The lady whose house I was living, made me large lunches, and I would divide it between my siblings. This way, I could relax knowing they had something to eat. Once social services found out I was stopping at my mother's, they forbid me. Nothing was going to stop me from going there, and when they found out I was still going against their wishes, they decided to discipline me. Now back then, discipline meant beating, and since the man of the foster house was a preacher, he would quote scriptures. "The Bible says, 'Spare the rod, and spoil the child.'"

And then he would beat me. This did not stop me, and after that beating, I ran away in an effort to be home with my real family. I did not understand or care that the Bible told this man to beat me, and as far as I was concerned, he was just like all the rest of the adults in my life, abusive.

I knew that I could not go home to stay even though I was only twelve. I had enough sense to know that if I tried to stay home, the

Social Services would only come and take me back. I stayed in the street and would sneak in and out of my mother's house to check on my siblings. When my mother asked any questions, I would say that the people I was with knew where I was. I never hung around too long. Because I knew the people were looking for me, and this would be the first place they would come. So after an hour or so, I would leave. My siblings would make leaving hard. They would tell me how much they wished I was still at home with them, but I would promise them that I would be back to see them soon.

In the street, it was survival of the fittest. I would steal food to eat or would eat at a friend's house. I began running with a gang of about eight boys around my age, and we would steal from toy stores, and I would take toys to my siblings. We would go into Laundromats and snatch unattended pocketbooks, into supermarkets for the cash registers, and to sporting events. Then the gang graduated to burglarizing stores. The burglaries started by accident. We had heard that this particular store was having a sale on knives, and we (the gang) wanted to buy some, but when we got there, the store was closed. Right then and there, we made the decision to come back later and break in. So it was decided that we would go to the movies and then return to break in and steal the knives to keep some and sale some. I was not living by any rules. Why should I since nobody else was, especially the adults? My father leaving me was against the rule, my mother drinking and running the streets was against the rule, and my stepfather abusing me on every level that I could be abused was against the rule. Why should I live by any rule?

Eventually, Social Services caught up with me. I was walking down the street with my mother when they pulled up beside us. I thought about running, but my mother told me not to. The man got out of the car and began talking with my mother. I heard him tell her that he would have to take me with him. My mother pleaded with him to let me stay with her and promised to make a life for me with her. The man from Social Services said it was not his decision but that it was a legal matter, and if she wanted me with her, she would have to go to court. After my mother realized that talking with this man would not get her anywhere, she turned to me and told me to go with him, and if I ran, it would only be harder for me. Then she promised she would go to court and get me home. I did not believe her even though her intentions were good. Her follow-through was not so good. I decided not to run but to go with the social worker. The people whose house I was placed in did not want me back, and the social worker thought if they moved me further away from my family, I would be better off. So they moved me to a place a lot farther away.

These people were not bad people, and the only thing I had against them was they were not my family, and I would only be satisfied with my family. The people I was placed with had a farm and a lot of land. They had one son who was older than me by a couple of years. Whenever they introduced us, he was always introduced as their real son, and I was the foster child, and I resented that. There was a funeral home we would drive by with the name of Foster's Funeral Home, and I thought this is where they probably took foster children when they died.

Back at the house, I had my own room, my own bed, and everything in it, but I could not enjoy it because I knew my family did not have it, and they were suffering. I felt as long as I did not enjoy these things, I could suffer with them.

Sometimes, I would not eat because I worried that my siblings were not eating. I would always find myself wondering about how my mother was doing. After a couple of months of not being allowed to visit them, I could not take it any longer. I began to make my plans to run away. The lady of the house would take me into the city along with her to shop. As we rode, I would make mental notes of different landmarks, buildings, trees, signs, etc. Finally, the day came when I would make my move. The lady of the house loved to watch her soap operas. She would send me to my room for a nap while she watched the soaps. This all played into my plans. I had my route pretty much down pat. I went into her room, took some money out of her purse, and jumped out of the window. She would be watching TV for hours, and that was enough time for me to get a good head start. As I walked passing landmark after landmark, all thoughts in my head were of seeing my family again.

After walking what seemed like forever, I finally reached my old neighborhood. I went to the house, and after looking around making sure it was clear, I went inside. There was my mother and my siblings. They were happy to see me, but they were not as happy to see me as I was to see them. My mother did not ask me any questions. She probably knew I had run away again. I gave her some of the money I stole and some to my siblings. It felt so good to be with them. I could not stay long because I knew the people I was living with had called and reported to the Social Services that I had run away. They were probably looking for me by now, so I had to go. It was back to the street and my old gang.

My mother was worried about me because the caseworker told her if I ran away again, they would send me to reform school. She began calling around members of the family to see if any of them would be willing to take me in, and there were no takers. She was so desperate that she called Florida in an effort to reach my real father, but that was to no avail.

Like I said, it was back to the street and a life of petty crimes. In the back of my mind, I knew the welfare people would catch up with me, but until they did, I would be on the run. I was able to duck the authorities for about a year. That was a year of eating hand to mouth and sleeping where I could lay my head. Sometimes, I would sleep at friend's houses and sometimes in cars on car lots and I have even slept under friends' houses on the ground. In that year, we committed a string of petty crimes. No matter what happened, I always looked after my mother and my siblings. When I stole something they needed like food, money, toys, and clothes, I would take it by the house and leave.

Reformed School

—◦◦◦—

Eventually, my delinquent life led me to the reform school. I had been through the foster care system, and after running away from one home after the other, the state had had enough. The judge committed me to the reform school as a ward of the state. I had heard tales about the reform school from guys that had been there. My lawyer told my mother that if I went there and behaved myself, I could be home in six months. I asked him when I got out, could I come home and stay with my mother. The lawyer said yeah. This was all I wanted, to be with my family, my mother. Once the lawyer said I could come back after six months and be with my mother, I was all right. I would go to this place and stay out of trouble, behave myself, and come home.

Once I got there, I did not know what to expect, but no matter what happens, I made up my mind. I was not going to get in any trouble. I would stay to myself. But in a place like that, although you want to stay away from problems and trouble, troubles had a way of finding you. I was fifteen years old and had started to smoke. I did not have any money, so I would bum a cigarette from time to time. In this place, a cigarette was like money. You would gamble for them and fight for them, and some of the weaker guys would do sexual favors for them. The state would give you a dollar canteen card at the first of the month, so whenever I bummed a cigarette, I always promised to give it back on the first and would.

In this place, there were gangs and cliques that ran together. Usually, these gangs made up of five or six guys, and they preyed on the weaker guys or the new guy. I was the new guy, and this one particular gang decided they wanted to try me. There was a separation of Blacks and Whites, not by rules or regulations of the school. Blacks just hung with Blacks, and Whites hung with Whites. There were a few White guys who wanted to hang with Black guys and were allowed to, but the Blacks would use them to run errands and used them for their canteen money. This gang that wanted to try me used one of their White guys to do their dirty work. This White guy wanted to make points with the gang, so he accepted the task of trying me.

In the beginning, he would do small things to harass me. He would jump the line in front of me, the chow line, canteen line, etc. I would not bite remembering I had to stay out of trouble if I wanted to get out of this place in six months and return to my family. But because I did not respond to his tactics, he thought I was weak, so he turned it up a notch. He would accidentally push past me and would not say sorry, letting me know he did not care, and if I did not like it, I could do something about it, he was trying to provoke me. In the dormitory, we had to make our beds. The aisle between the beds was so narrow that only one could fit in it to make up the side. One morning, I was in the aisle, and he pushed me out of the way so he could tuck in his blankets. I still refused to fight him, I just looked at him, and he just knew I was a punk now. He did not realize I was no punk but that I just did not want any trouble.

One day, we had finished our workday and had gone back to our cottage. Once inside, we had recreation time. In the recreation room, we had a pool table, Ping-Pong table, and card tables. I was playing cards. In order to shoot pool, you had to put your name on a list. If you won, you could continue playing until you lost. Now this guy who was giving me a hard time was a good player, and he had won about ten games in a row. When out of nowhere, this kid beats him, a kid who could not play pool at all. After he lost, all the guys started laughing and teasing him. He noticed I was laughing, came over, and punched me on the side of my head. That was it. I pushed myself away from the table and began by punching him in the mouth. He was in shock. Then I hit him a few times about his face before they pulled me off him. We had white T-shirts on, and his was bloody, and I did not have to worry about him bothering me again after that. I began to realize that I was not going to be able to stay out of trouble if it meant I would have to let these guys run all over me. I did not have any money except the dollar I received once a month. I smoked, I liked snacks, and nobody ever came for a visit from home or sent me any money. I was on my own.

On my own, it seemed to me I have been on my own since I was born. Now here in this reform school, it rang true more than ever. The word *reform* was in question. Reformed to what? Would being reformed make you better or make you harder? In my case, I became harder. I had to be harder to survive. The staff were racists, sadistic, and abusive. Not only did you have to survive among your peers but those on the staff also. The staff would beat you up until you fell, and then they would kick and stomp you, and all this was done in front of the boys and other staff members. The boys would rate the staff members that gave the best "stomp job," meaning which staff member beat you up the worst. Usually, any stomp job victim that ended up in the on-site infirmary, that staff member got the highest rating. There was no real protection for any of us. We had to protect ourselves. If you did not know how to fight, you had to learn and learn fast.

After my fight with that guy, they did not stop feeling me out, but they knew I could fight. There were weaker guys who did not have any fight in them, and they were taken advantage of. I always had a heart for the underdog. I guess because I was one. Some of these guys would hang around me, they wanted to be my friend, and I would befriend them. The other guys would leave them alone once they saw them with me. As a result of these friendships, the weaker guys would buy me cigarettes and snacks. I never befriended them for this reason, but once they started buying me stuff, I could not say no. I was not in any position to say no. We became friends and played ball and cards and hung out together. Some of them had visitors on a regular basis, and often, their parents would call me over to picnic with them. One father knew that I was protecting his son. He never said it, but he knew, so he would put money in my account so

I would keep being friends with his son. It was not a deal I sat down and drew up, but it worked out my way.

One day, a substitute house leader came into the cottage to relieve the regular leader who had gone on vacation. The substitute wanted to establish his leadership and was not going to take any stuff from us. We were all in the recreation room when he shut down all activities and called our attention to him. He started out saying, "I might be new here, but I am not taking anything off of any of you." He went on to say how he can handle his fists and if anyone of us thought they could take him to step forward. He said that whoever stepped up and got the best of him, he would not turn them in. Jokingly, I raised my hand and said, "I think I can take you." I had a sense of humor, and that was all I was doing—joking. This man got angry and said, "Come on up if you think you can handle me. Come on." I saw that he thought I was serious, and I began to try to tell him I was just playing around. He insisted that I come with him into the locker room and that if I won, he would not turn me in. I was still pleading with him as he led me to the locker room. He wanted to establish himself so bad and planned on making an example of me. Once inside the locker room, he turned without warning and grabbed me by my collar with both hands. My reflex kicked in, and I grabbed him back. I had a real tight grip on him, and I began to sling him into the lockers. I slung him into one locker after another. Each time he hit the locker, there was a loud clanking noise.

I finally let go, and he ran out of the cottage. I knew I was in trouble, not just trouble but real big trouble. He had lied when he said he would not turn me in. Once he ran outside, I knew he was running to tell on me. I went back to the recreation area. Everybody was looking at me. They did not know what went down, but they heard all the noise, and I was the only one to return. They knew to that I was in real big trouble. When the man returned, he had two other men with him. One was the headman, the superintendent of the school. The superintendent was known for giving out decent "stomp jobs," and I was about to find out. He did not say anything to me. He slapped me in the face, but I did not go down. Then he began punching me with his fists. After a few hits in the face, I went down, and then the kicking and stomping began. The other man that came with them was just standing there until I went down, and then he joined in and began kicking and stomping me also. Once they finished, I was told to put my chair facing the wall. The next day, they passed out my punishment. For thirty days, I was not allowed to smoke and participate in any recreation room activities, and I was to sit facing the wall. Even though I was just joking, this incident added to my reputation, but it also added to my time there. I could forget about getting out in six months.

My sense of humor got me into a lot of trouble while I was here. It was my way of keeping the attention off me and onto someone else. It was also my attempt of being accepted. I figured people would like me if I made them laugh. Like I said, my sense of humor got me in trouble. A few times, it got me beat up really bad like the time in the locker room with the substitute father. That beating resulted in me spending a night in the infirmary.

There was one other incident that landed me in the infirmary, but it was for a longer stay. It was bedtime, and the night watchman had taken us to the dormitory and saw to it that all of us were in our beds, and the lights were out. This particular night, the watchman decided to talk some trash to us before he turned the lights out. It seemed to be all about intimidation, everybody wanted to intimidate us, and this watchman was no different. The only problem was his trash talking and the fact he had only one arm. He was walking up and down the aisle, talking trash with his one arm. He talked about how he would catch anybody who tried to escape and what he would do to them once he caught them. He went on and on. This was during the sixties, and there was a very popular television program called *The Fugitive*. The story line was about this doctor who was falsely accused of murdering his wife, and there was a one-arm man who could prove his innocence. The character (the doctor) was Richard Kimble, and he escaped to go hunt for the one-arm man.

As the night watchman walked by my bed and got up front, I turned my head toward the wall and said, "Oh, shut up! Richard Kimble is looking for you." Well, everybody in the dormitory broke out in laughter. Everybody that is, except for the night watchman.

He stood there turning redder and redder until I thought he would explode. Finally, he screamed, "Everybody up!" He ordered us to stand at the head of our bunks with our hands placed behind our head. He threatened that we would stand there in that position until he found out who said that. Everybody knew I said it, but nobody wanted the reputation of being a squealer, and at this point, I was really counting on that. Guys were still laughing at my joke. When one of them would look at the watchman, they would laugh. I wish they would not keep laughing and just let it go because every time, it made him angrier, and woe be it on the poor guy when he found out who said it. That poor guy was me.

We had been standing in that same position for about an hour or so with our hands behind our head. The watchman was going in and out of the dormitory, and each time he came in, he would ask, "Are you tired yet?" He said that we would stay in this position until someone talked. By now, all the humor had left the building. The guys were not laughing now, their arms were hurting, and they wanted to go to bed, but they did not want to squeal. They were probably praying to God that I would step out and own up to it. If that was what they were thinking, they could forget that prayer. I was not going to step up. I did not care if my arms fell off. This happened over forty years ago, and if they waited for me to man up, we would still be standing there in our fifties.

The code of not being a squealer did not extend to everyone. The Black guys lived more by this creed than the White guys. I noticed two White guys whispering back and forth and looking at me, and I knew they were up to something. One of the guys was tall, and the other was about my size. When the night watchman came back in and asked if anyone was ready to talk, the shorter guy raised his hand, and the watchman took him out to the foyer. It was my turn to change colors now, and I knew I was in for it, and everybody in that dormitory knew I was in for it. There was a dead silence in that place. The guys gave me looks of pity as if to say, "Boy, I feel sorry for you." When the watchman returned with his squealer in tow, he told everyone to get in bed except for bed number sixteen, which was my bed number, and they did. There I was standing alone with my hand behind my head, and he stopped directly in front of me. He stared for a moment, and I could see the rage in his eyes, the hate, and the anger. Finally, he said, "Oh, Richard Kimble is looking for me?" I wish he had not said that because some of the guys started laughing again and that only added to this man's anger. He punched me as hard as he could in the pit of my stomach. With my hands behind my head, I could not defend myself, and I was wide open for that punch. I double over from the impact, and he told me to stand back up and resume the position. He repeated his question.

"So Richard Kimble is looking for me?"

This time, he punched me in the face. I went back but did not go down. Again, I was told to place my hands behind my head. I was bleeding from my mouth. The punch in the face busted my lip, and I could taste blood. I stood back up with my hands behind my head. I could feel my anger rising in me. There was nothing I could do but just stare him in the face. I wanted him to see the anger in my eyes.

After those two punches, I thought that was it. The watchman left. I was still standing in the same position, and I figured he would leave me there for a while to teach me a lesson and then allow me to go to bed. I was wrong. He was gone about a half hour and then came back. He took me by my arm and led me out of the dormitory. As I passed by each bunk, the guys had this look of pity again. Once outside, I noticed there were two other men waiting. There were twelve cottages on the grounds, and there was one night watchman for every two, so there were six watchmen altogether. He had gone and summoned two of the watchmen to help him. They led me down the steps that led directly into the locker area, the same locker room where I had the earlier incident with the substitute housefather.

I was told to place my hands against the wall and to run in place. As I was running in place with one man on each side, the beating began. Each man took turns punching me in my side, punching me in the rib cage. I was told to keep running. I was determined that there were two things I was not going to do. One, I was not going to cry, and two, I was not going down. I was able to do the first. I did not cry, but with them punching my side and face, the pain was too much, and I went down. Then the "stomp job" began. They started

26

kicking and stomping me like I was an animal. They did not care where their kicks landed—face, side, or back. I balled up in a knot in an effort to protect myself from all the blows. Then I was told to squat and walk like a duck. As I swaddled back and forth like a duck, the kicking and punching continued. I was bleeding from my eyes, nose, and mouth. My left eye was swollen shut. I think they stopped beating me because they were just too tired to continue. These three men had punched, kicked, and stomped me so much that they wore themselves out. All the while, they kept saying, "We are going to teach this nigger who to mess with. We are going to teach this nigger a lesson." They took me back to the dormitory and told me to go to bed. As I walked toward my bed, I could barely see through my swollen eyes, but I managed to pause at the foot of the bed of the guy who ratted on me and then kept walking. The guys that were still up were looking at me, and I thought I must be bad off because they were cringing when they saw my face. I got into my bunk. My shirt was so bloody. I had to take it off, and I laid there in silence, thinking how I was going to get the rat. Finally, I went off to sleep.

The next morning, I discovered dried blood all over the pillowcase, my left eye was closed tight from the swelling, and my rib cage hurt. I could barely get myself out of bed. I managed to make up my bed after changing the linen and made my way downstairs. I took a look in the mirror, and I saw why the guys cringed when they saw me. I was beat up kind of bad. Once the regular housefather saw me, he was a decent man, he ordered me to be taken to the infirmary at once. Two of the guys accompanied me there. When I got there, I found out I had cracked ribs, and they gave me some pain medicine and kept me there for a few days until the swelling went down. As I lay in that hospital bed as a result of a beating I received from three grown men who were never held accountable, did anybody in authority asks, "What did this child do that he deserved to be beaten like this?" The answer is "no." The authorities said I was incorrigible and that I had to be broken by any means necessary. This was the label on me. Instead of being broken, I hardened. I dug my heels in deeper against those in authority over me. It did not start here in the reform school. It started from the day I became conscious that my father left me. It started when my stepfather kicked and beat me. It started when he called me a "bigheaded bastard" or a Black SOB. It started when my stepfather would say to my mother, "If you are going out, you better take this MF with you." My resentment against any authority figure started when I was not allowed to eat food that my stepfather bought. I would watch him feed his biological children, and he would not feed me, and I was eight years old at the time. If I was incorrigible, it was because I was raised to be. I was not born incorrigible. I was taught.

When I got out of the hospital, I had something to attend to, the rat. There was a reason why you did not want to rat. You could get beat up for ratting. I did not write the rule book, but I lived by it in this place. I had a running mate who became my friend in order to keep me from beating him up. A while back, he and his then partner double-teamed and beat me up. I knew I could handle him but was not so sure about his partner. I knew I could not handle the two of them, but I never forgot about that double-teaming. The time came for his partner to go home, leaving him alone and giving me an open to get some pay back. He immediately started giving me cigarettes and asking me to partner up with him in card games. I eventually let it go, and we became friends. So together, we were going to get this rat. We decided to get him in the dorm after the lights went out.

That night, we all went to bed, and the watchmen turned out the lights. We waited for about an hour and got up and snuck up on the guy's bed. I was on one side and my partner on the other, and we found the guy asleep. I hit him first. Then my partner joined in. We did not beat him bad but just enough for him to get the message— do not be a rat. The next morning, the rat's friend ratted on me but not on my partner. I was put on report for the housefather to see. Even though the housefather was a fair man, the rat was his favorite boy, and he did not like anybody messing with him. After reading the report, he came to me and slapped me around a little. I was used to being punched, kicked, and stomped, so these few slaps did not faze me. I was also put on restriction, which meant sitting in the chair facing the wall. He said two weeks, but he took me off after a few days. Like I said, he was a fair man. In fact, before I left, I became his favorite. He would come to get me on a Saturday and ride around the grounds just to talk to me. He taught me how to play bridge, and we actually became close. He was the one I give credit to for finally getting me out of that place.

There were a lot of guys there that were deemed incorrigible, and they (the State) came up with this place we called the Junior State Penitentiary. Guys the state thought were a lost cause would be sent there until their eighteenth birthday. The guys who was on the list (there was no doubt I was on it) would be woken up early while everyone else was sleeping, and you would not see him anymore. I know I was a candidate for this list, and I lost many hours of sleep waiting for them to come for me. One requirement for going to the new place was if you were at the reform school for more than a year. I had been here for over a year. They had a committee that met every month, and after a boy had been there for four months with good behavior, he would go before the board. If he had been really outstanding, the committee would let him go home. Now if you had been misbehaving, the committee would meet with you, review your case, and give you another month, sometimes two depending on how bad your conduct had been.

I had been before the board seven times and turned down for release each time. I just knew I would be sent to this Junior State Penitentiary. After I was turned down the last time, I decided to change my ways. I was sixteen coming up on seventeen, and if I was sent to the other place, I would be there until my eighteenth birthday. I did not want that, so I saw the light and began to change my behavior. It was not that hard. Most of the trouble I got into was because of fighting, and I won a lot of the fights I got into. The guys would not bother me. The weaker guys I protected from the bullies kept me in cigarettes and snacks, and their fathers who did not want their sons coming home a punk would put a few dollars in my canteen account. So behaving was not that bad, and I was tired of this place and wanted to go home. I received two letters from my mother with a dollar in each one. I stayed in the reform school for sixteen months. With the government giving me sixteen dollars and the two dollars from my mother made a total of eighteen dollars to see me through those sixteen months. I never blamed my mother because I did not expect much from her because she did not have much. At this point in my life, I placed all the blame on my father for leaving the family.

It is really important that if one of your children gets themselves in trouble that you support them. Now supporting them does not mean you uphold what they did, but even though they made a mistake, it just shows you still love them. When I went before the committee for the last time, after staying out of trouble, I was told I could go home, but there would be two conditions that had to happen before I could leave. First, I had to find a job, and second, someone besides my mother would have to allow me to come to their home. With these conditions, I really did not feel like I was going to go home. I did not want to go to a foster home. I really wanted to be with my mother, my sisters, and my brothers. I was told if I did not meet these conditions, I would be until I turned eighteen and released on my own. I was tired of this place and did not want to stay another year.

The next day, a state social worker took me into the city. He told me that if I did not secure a job and a place or a home that would take me in, I would be taken back to the reform school until I did. I had that hopeless feeling in the pit of my stomach that I would be there until I was grown. Once we got into the city, the social worker bought a local newspaper, and we began to look through the want ads. We went to a couple of offices only to be turned away for one reason or another. I was too young, not enough experience, or not wanting to take a chance on someone just getting out of the reform school. Still looking in the paper, we saw an ad for a janitor at a hospital and decided to try that one. When we got to the hospital, the social worker told me that if my age came up to tell them I was seventeen and would be eighteen that November, in other words lie. I was thinking if I do not get this job, it is back to the reform school I go, so I said okay. The question came up. I lied and got the job. Now half of my battle was over.

The social worker asked me if I had any ideas. *Do I have any ideas? You are the social worker*, I thought to myself. *You are the one that is supposed to have an idea. I have been locked up in reform school for almost two years, no visitors, no letters, or anything. How was I supposed to have an idea of where to stay?*

The only people I could think of that might take me in were my grandparents. So we drove to their home. My grandmother was not home. She was out shopping, but my grandpa was there, and he let us in. My grandpa was happy to see me. He made me feel good because it had been a long time since anybody said to me, "It is good to see you." We sat and made small talk, waiting for my grandmother to come home. Even though we told my grandpa what was going on with me, I knew he would say yes or no without hearing from Grandma. We heard a car pulling up in the driveway. It was Grandma. My grandpa told me to hide so we could surprise her. I went into the kitchen. Once she came in the house, I came out. She took one look at me and screamed. She put her arms around me and asked, "How have you been, baby?" I said okay. She cradled my face in the palms of her hands and said how good it was to see me. She was so happy and surprised to see me that she had not noticed the social worker.

After the introduction was done, it was now time to get down to why I was here, and we all sat down. The social worker did most of the talking. He told them where I had been for the past sixteen months. He explained the only conditions in which the state would release me. He told them what would happen to me if these conditions were not met. He told them about the job at the hospital and that the only thing left was finding me a place to stay. The social worker did a good job of selling me, but my grandmother was already sold the moment she saw me. My grandparents had a heart for me, and they agreed that they would take me in. I could not believe it! I'm coming home! I'm the leaving reform school.

The Stockades of Europe

In looking back on this life, I am convinced that like many others, we are products of our environment. Does this mean if we are born in the ghetto we are doomed to stay there? No, it does not. What it means is until I realized what was controlling my actions, my thoughts, and my behavior, I will continue to carry on what the Bible refers to as "generation curses." I will keep repeating my father's sins and his father before him. It may sound a bit like I have studied psychology or something. I did take Psychology 101 in college as an elective and received an A, but I still do not speak as an expert. I only speak to my own experience through continual self-inventory and self-examination. I do not want to come off as someone who offers a lot of excuses and/or one who is passing blame. One thing I have found during the examining of oneself is that a vast majority of the things that have happened in my life have been my fault, and no one else can be blamed. Of course, there are things that happened to me that were not my fault but allowed those things that caused me to do the things I did that were my fault.

Just one of many issues was a deep distaste for any authority figure. It was my experience as a child that anyone that had charge over me abused me in one way or another. I learned not to trust anyone in authority because they would eventually abuse that authority. Now with this deep-seeded resentment against authority figures, I went out and joined the Army in July 1969. As a private, everyone had charge over you. The Army and I got off to a great start. I sailed through basic training mainly because of the ever-present threat of doing it all over again if you messed up.

My real problem did not start until I went to Germany. This was during the Civil Rights era, which included the era of Dr. Martin Luther King vs. Minister Malcolm X and their different philosophies. I was not caught up in the civil rights struggle. At the time, I was too busy discovering women. I was nineteen and had not had a lot of experience with the ladies. I went AWOL a lot to gain more experience, and the women of Germany were more than willing to teach me. I did not go AWOL for any long length of time. The longest period was about three days, and the Army would punish me with extra duty and restriction to company area and an Article 15, which resulted in a fine. Like I said at the time, I was not caught up in the civil rights movement, but little did I know I would be thrust in the middle of it without my consent.

It was strange how it all started. I was stationed in Germany outside of Munich and was coming back to the barracks after being AWOL for two days. As I was walking through the gate, I was met by my company commander. He informed me that I was summoned to headquarters. I remember thinking, *The General wants to see me for going AWOL, and the Army must be really tired of my stuff.* The captain led me across the post and up to HQ and never spoke a word. He would look back periodically to make sure I was still following him. As I have said, I was not an ideal soldier. I went AWOL a lot and refused to cut my hair, but that was the extent of my misbehaving. Now I am about to come face-to-face with the general, and I am thinking court-martial to be sure, a summary at best.

As the captain and I, entered the general's office through two giant doors, the general sat there behind his oak desk. I did not see the two SID agents that fell in behind me as we entered the office. I was immediately handcuffed. All I was told was that I was under arrest. I was not told what the charge was, only that I was under arrest. But I knew the charges must be going AWOL and disobeying the order to cut my Afro. I thought this was a bit extreme, but I dismissed that thought. I was taken to the Nuremberg stockade. I asked what was I being charged with and was informed that the

Army had forty-eight hours to notify me of the charges. I am still thinking AWOL. A few days later, I had a visit from my captain. He came to read me the charges. He took out a stack of legal papers and began reading from them.

He read that on June 20, 1970, Pvt. Ronald L. Warren did willfully attempt to murder Captain So-and-So (I forgot the name). He read on that on June 20, 1970, Pvt. Ronald L. Warren did willfully attempt to murder Lieutenant So-and-So. I stood there at my cell door and listened to the captain read off twenty-three accounts of attempts of murder, nineteen accounts of destroying government property, ten counts of conspiracy, and five counts of assaults. My summary court-martial went straight to general court-martial. I stood there in shock. I could not believe what I was hearing. I honestly did not have a clue what this was all about.

It was not until my military lawyer came to see me did I began to understand what this was all about. All this stuff began because of my Afro. The general ruled that Blacks could wear Afros if we kept them two inches on the side and three inches on top and well-groomed. On the night of June 20, 1970, a group of Black soldiers decided to go to the general and put in a formal request that the Army bring in Afro products. Johnson and Johnson had a line of products designed to keep your Afro well-groomed—shampoo, hair spray, large combs, hair picks, etc. Since we were ordered to keep our hair well-groomed, it was only fair that we have the products needed to abide by the general's orders.

I would like to repeat myself. I was not the ideal soldier and with my personal issues (deep resentment of all authority), I probably should not have been in the Army in the first place. I did not blame the Army. In fact, despite it all, I learned a great deal in the military. I am simply writing this because it happened, and it is a part of my history.

A group of Black soldiers decided to march over to HQ and meet with the general. We all filed into the assembly hall (there were over four hundred soldiers) and took seats, and I sat with a group from my company up front. Nothing was really planned. There was no appointed spokesman for the group. We had discussed the issue and decided to meet with the general. I was surprised at the number of soldiers that were there. I guess some were just standing around when they saw us marching and decided to join the rally. They did not know what it was all about but figured it must concern them because we were all Black.

A door opened. We were all expecting the general to walk in, but it was the colonel instead. The room got quiet. The colonel announced that the general would not be addressing us but that he would gladly listen and take our concerns to him. The crowd got loud and shouted their disappointment that the general did not care enough to meet with us. There was a lot of racial tension during this time, and the group saw with the general not showing up as another way of saying we were not important. I sort of felt the mood of the crowd, stood up, and said, "We do not want to talk to you 'the colonel.' We want to meet with the general." I said that, meaning we would like to meet with the general when he was available. But as if on cue, after I made that statement, the crowd began exiting the hall. As I walked out, I looked back at the colonel, and he looked at me. Later, I found out that statement marked me a leader.

As we continued to file out, everybody went their separate ways back to their respective companies. I went back along with the guys from my company to our barracks. The next day, I woke up to find out that all hell had broken out the night before after the meeting ended. The tension was high, but I never knew how high. Some of the soldiers did not return to their barracks. They went on a rampage. They broke into the ammo dump, stole grenades, and began tossing them around the post. One grenade was tossed into a mess hall where twenty-three White soldiers were eating. A grenade was tossed into the motor pool exploding diesel fuel and causing other damages. Because I opened my rebellious mouth that night in the meeting hall, telling the colonel we did not care to talk with him, the crowd reacted by getting up (as if on cue) and walked out marking me as a leader. The way the Army thought, either I did it, I knew who did it or had given the orders to do it. They were wrong on all accounts, but here I was in the stockade charged with these horrible crimes and facing life in prison.

The captain gave me a copy of my official charges. I must have read them a thousand times before it sunk in that this was really happening. It took a few days to adjust to life in the stockade. I just kept telling myself I did not do it, and somehow, someway, the truth would come out, and I will be set free.

As the word began to spread throughout the stockades as to my charges, I gained notoriety within the stockade. I was kept away from the general population in solitary confinement. This only added to my false reputation. The case received a lot of media attention, *Jet* magazine, *Ebony*, from newspapers throughout both Europe and the United States. People have a tendency to believe what they read in the papers or see on television. They thought if it made the paper or was on television, then it must be true. This was in the aftermath of the assassination of President John F. Kennedy, Senator Robert Kennedy, Dr. Martin Luther King, and Minister Malcolm X. Black people were desperate for a leader. Please do not get me wrong because I am not considering myself among these great, great men. What I am trying or attempting to do is set the stage as it were in these times. People were looking for leaders anywhere they could find them. They saw the problems but could not do anything about them, and so as soon as someone came along that was outspoken against the injustices, the people would jump on the bandwagon. Just to show the desperation of many people for a leader, after reading the papers and watching TV, they decided I must be the one. I must be their new leader, me a leader, and all I ever did was to go AWOL a few times and refused to cut my hair. I was not making any kind of political statement by doing this. I was nineteen years old, and I went AWOL just to spend more time with the ladies, and I did not cut my Afro because the ladies liked playing in it. For me, it was all about the ladies.

I, myself, knew the truth, and the truth was I was no leader, and I am here on false charges, but no matter what you say, people will believe what they want to believe. They all believed that everyone here in prison had been falsely accused. This made it hard on the truly innocent. I was confined to my cell twenty-two hours a day at the beginning and let out for recreation one hour in the morning and one hour in the evening. I would spend this time in the yards shooting hoops. While in the yard, other prisoners would call out to me by my name. Most of the time, they would shout antiestablishment slogans "Brother Ron, power to the people" and "Right on, Brother Ron, right on." I could see fear in some of the guard's eyes. These responses only serve to keep me physically away from the rest of the prison population. I guess this was when I started tripping. The term *tripping* came about during the time of LSD and acid. When someone would say something that was ridiculous or impossible, one would say, "Oh, he is tripping." Even though I knew it was not true, I began to trip on all this attention and play the part of a Black militant leader. I had to do something that would take my mind off my dire situation, and this new role was the answer.

The way I figured, if I am going to play the role of a leader, I needed to study other leaders and their overall philosophies. I began to read books by Minister Malcolm X, Eldridge Cleaver, Huey Newton, Bobby Seale, H. Rap Brown, and Stokley Carmichael. When I read where Malcolm was quoted saying that he would not take up arms against you, but if you took up arms against him, he would defend himself. I thought, *Right on, brother.* This became my creed. I would defend myself if attacked. I would not be the attacker, but if attacked, I would be the defender. I did finally get around to studying Dr. King, but at the time, his philosophy of turning the other cheek was too far from mine. As I studied, I found myself so immersed in my reading that I did not have time to be confrontational with the guards for weeks. I would just stay in my cell and read. One day, I was totally surprised when they came and told me that they were going to move me into the general population. I was shocked. The time I spent studying led them to believe I had calmed down, and it would be okay to put me in with the general population.

It felt good to be with the brothers. It was like being freed in jail. I could talk, eat, and interact with other inmates, and it was great. I was still on this power trip where I was a leader, and so I continued my studies. The brothers would come to me with their problems and listen intently to my advice. I spent most of my time talking about the struggle of the Black man and how we must educate ourselves and prepare ourselves for the day we would return home and join in the struggle. In studying and reading about the civil rights movement, it became my vision to prepare myself to join the struggle when I returned to the states.

In the general population, I kept a low profile. Not only was I getting a lot of attention from the inmates, but also the guards kept their eyes on me. Whenever they made their rounds, they made sure they checked on me. I always had five or six inmates around my bunk, and when the guards came by, they would stop talking. This kept the guards on alert. There were times when we would have a test of will between the guards and me that more times than not would lead to me being put in solitary confinement. You see, I had this reputation to live up to, as it went, don't mess with Brother Ron because he is not going to back down. I tried to stay out of confrontations with the guards, but sometimes, it was unavoidable. One time, I was in the yard playing basketball when the guards announced it was time to go inside. The game was close to ending, and I asked the guard to give us the time to finish. Some of the guards would have allowed us to finish, but these guards were not willing. The rest of the inmates were waiting for me to tell them what to do. I said let's finish the game, and we continued to play. The guards sent for the riot squad (we called them the Goon Squad). Once the riot squad showed up, the inmates stopped playing and fell in line to go inside. I kept on shooting the ball in defiance, and the squad lifted me up in the air, and when my feet touched down, I was in the isolation cell all alone and without my mattress, which was removed as punishment. The guard whom I defied came by to taunt me. I lost my smoking privileges to boot. In the morning at breakfast, an inmate would slide my tray under my cell door and whisper to check between the slices of toast. I looked, and there between the slices of toast were three cigarettes and matches. Sometimes, they would put small pieces of hash in between the bread.

Even though I was doing all I could to keep my mind off of my situation, there were times when my own reality would sink in. Just as the inmates believed I was the person they read about in the paper and saw on television, there were probably even many more people outside the stockade who believed it also. There were times when I thought I was the only one who knew I was innocent. Since my lawyer was appointed by the Army, I really did not think he was completely in my corner. After all, he was an officer in the Army, and he was a part of the same system that had imprisoned me. During these moments of realizing, my situation caused me to act out and fueled my disputes with the prison guards.

After being confined in the stockade in Nuremburg a couple of months, my lawyer came to visit me. He bought me some news that day that still rings in my ears when I think about it. My lawyer told me that the Army was seeking the maximum sentence in my case. "What is that?" I asked. He said the Army is asking that I receive 195 years in prison, forfeit all pay, and reduced to the rank of private (I remember thinking the joke is on them because I am already a private) and that my sentence be carried out at Fort Leavenworth. I was glad to be sitting down at the time or I would have fallen.

After my interview with my lawyer, I was taken back to my cell. Once in the cell, I sat on the bunk, and all kinds of thoughts flooded my mind, seemingly all at once. One hundred and ninety-five years in prison took center stage in my mind. I may be tripping on all this, but the Army was not. They were serious. They are going to try to stick these charges on me. The Army was under a lot of pressure to convict me. Even though I knew I was innocent, doubt began to sink in, and maybe just being innocent would not be enough to free me. But the truth was all I had on my side. My life is in the hands of the truth, and the truth is "I did not do it!"

The media continued to portray me as a Black militant, which led to the rumors that I was connected to the then militant group, the Black Panthers. I was reading the paper one morning when a headline grabbed my attention, "Black Panther Leader, Mrs. Kathleen Cleaver, to Visit Private Warren." I began to read the story. It said that Mrs. Cleaver, wife of Black Panther's cofounder, Eldridge Cleaver, was visiting Germany in an effort to gain an interview with Pvt. Ronald L. Warren. Then the article went on to say that Private Warren was in the stockade charged with, and it went on to say what I was charged with. Every article written about me either started with or ended with what I was charged with. The article went on to say that Mrs. Cleaver was not allowed to leave the airport. Her attempt to visit me did not help my case. Even though I appreciated her desire to come to my aid, her visit gave fuel to the Army's lie that I was a Black Panther. If there was anyone who believed I was not a Panther would believe I was after reading the paper.

At this point, the Army's speculation that I was connected to the Panther Party was just that, pure speculation, but after Mrs. Cleaver's attempted visit, they were now convinced. This action started me on my tour of all the stockades of Europe. After denying her a visitation with me, the next story was that in retaliation. The Black Panthers planned to bust me out of the stockade. So the Army began to transfer me from stockade to stockade in an effort to prevent my escape. My transfers would take place randomly, early morning, midday, or late at night. I never knew when they would come to my isolation cell and tell me to pack it up. I would be housed at a stockade one or two weeks before the Army would transfer me. My case seemed to have taken on a life of its own and I didn't know what would happen next. It had made me out to be an attempted murderer. It had asked that I receive 195 years at hard labor. It had me connected to the Black Panther Party. It had even gone so far as to have me being busted out of jail. It even had me playing the role of a militant. So in essence, my own actions were helping their case. If I was tripping before, the fashion in which the Army continued to really had me tripping.

The Army was not taking any chances. If the Panthers came after me, they would be ready for them. Let me lay out for you how far they went in an all-out effort to prevent my escape. I already told you how they would transfer me at all times of the day or night. When they came to get me, they came with a small platoon of twenty heavily armed soldiers. I would be placed in handcuffs and leg irons and positioned in the middle of them, ten soldiers in the front and ten bringing up the rear. I would be taken out into the yard to a waiting army bus. There were more armed troops in the yard. There were four sedans and four soldiers in each. There were two motorcycles and a helicopter overhead. (Did I mention I was innocent that the most I had ever done was to go AWOL?) The twenty soldiers that were escorting me out got on the bus along with me. They seated me in the middle of the bus, and they took their seats all around me. As the gate opened, the two motorcycles took the lead followed by two sedans, the bus carrying me, and the other two sedans bringing up the rear. The helicopters hovered overhead. I remember thinking that, hell, I was praying that if the Black Panthers had any thought of busting me out, they would change their minds. If they did not and tried it, a small war would break out, and if that happened, there would be a great chance I would be hurt or killed especially since I was chained and did not have any way to defend myself.

The soldiers were under orders not to converse with me and that I was dangerous. I believe I saw some fear in the eyes of some of them. It was not a fear of me but a fear of what would happen if the Panthers showed up. They believed what they read in the paper that they were actually transporting a Black Panther, and I looked, acted, and spoke like one (or their idea of a Panther). They were under orders not to talk to me, but I was not under orders not to talk to them. I would make some remarks to the Black soldiers in reference to their loyalty and how misplaced it was or that I can't believe the Army is going through all this and that I was innocent. For the most part, they obeyed their orders, but they would laugh at a joke or tell me to shut up if I said something they did not find funny. They even threatened to tape my mouth if I did not shut up. I remember that during one transfer, I told them I had to go to the restroom. I really did not have to go, but as I said, I was power tripping and wanted to see how they would handle my request and the situation. After complaining that I had to go bad, they stopped at what was a German restaurant. The soldiers in the sedans got out and entered the restaurant, and some went around the outside. They even went into other stores that were close to the restaurant. After checking everything out, the all clear was radioed to the troops on the bus. They filed off in columns of two, and I was brought off the bus and placed in the middle. I looked up at the helicopter overhead. It just hovered there about a hundred or so yards overhead. The people on the street were looking at the scene wide-eyed, especially the patrons inside the restaurant. I saw fear in their faces and thought to myself if I yelled

"Boo!" that I would not be the only one in need of the restroom. My next thought if I did that is I would get myself shot, so with all the guns around me, I better not make any sudden moves.

Whenever I arrived at a stockade, the brothers would welcome me. They would be at the fence yelling, "Right on, Brother Ron! Power to the people!" I would raise my fists in chains and yell back to them, "Right on!" They (the soldiers) would hurry me into the building, and I would be placed immediately in solitary confinement. Once the word went through the stockade I was there (especially the dining hall), the brothers began to look out for me. They made sure I had cigarettes and snacks, and they would even sneak hashish to me usually between my bread on the food tray that was slipped under my cell door. Some of the Black guards looked out for me. They would get my mail out uncensored and bring me books. There would be outbreaks between Blacks and Whites, and before it got out of hand, they would bring me up to help settle the situation. I was not a Black Panther, but I probably would have made a good one if I decided to join. I was not used to getting any attention growing up. I always felt that I did not matter that I was a nobody. But now here, I was getting attention, and I was somebody, and to be honest, I was enjoying it.

I was being held in what was called pretrial confinement, as my day in court was drawing near. My lawyer and I met to discuss my defense and what actual evidence the Army had against me. There were two key pieces of evidence. One, they (the Army) had a soldier who testified that he saw me making a Molotov cocktail, and two, they had a group made up of about twenty White guys from my company who said I had threatened them. Everything else the Army had was minor.

The day finally came for my pretrial, and my usual entourage was here to pick me up. Once we arrived at the courthouse, I was whisked inside. My lawyer was already in the courtroom, and I was led over to the table and took a seat beside him. My lawyer asked if I was nervous, and I said, "Yes, I was." He told me to relax and reminded me that this was just a preliminary just to see if the Army had enough evidence to go forward with a trial. The process had begun, and the Army called their first witness, the man who said he saw me making a firebomb. The first thing they asked was if he could identify Pvt. Ronald Warren, and this man pointed directly at me without any hesitation. This was strange because I had never seen this man in my life. After him, the Army began to bring in the White soldiers who were supposed to have been threatened by me. They came in one after the other and pretty much said the same thing, I had threatened them. My lawyer asked them if I threatened them as a group or did I go from one to the other with my threat. They said I had threatened them as a group. My lawyer said, "You are all soldiers in the United States Army, and one man threatens you as a group, and you were actually afraid." My lawyer kind of made them look rather ridiculous. After that cross-examining, the only evidence remaining was the man who said he saw me making a firebomb. I was taken back to the stockade to wait and see if the Army would pursue the trial. My lawyer told me that they may go to trial but that the Army's case was not that strong. For the first time in a long time, I felt some hope.

Back at the stockade, it was the same thing. I was living the life of a celebrity, but it was not fun anymore. My case had my attention. I had calmed down even though I had grown men seeking my advice and actually taking it. My concentration was on my situation. The officials still kept me in solitary confinement. They were under orders to do so, but they did not treat me badly. For the next month, I stayed out of trouble and to myself. I was going over in my mind again and again how could this total stranger say he saw me making a firebomb and point me out to the court. He was lying, but why? He must have been told to say this. Not only was he told to lie, he must have been shown a picture of me to back up his lie. The Army was under a lot of pressure to convict somebody of these crimes. I would not put it past them (the Army) to have done this. I could not prove any of this, and I would like to think they would not do it, but what other explanation could have been?

One evening, I was in the yard, smoking a cigarette, when I was summoned upstairs to the office. I was told I had a phone call from my lawyer. My heart stopped. I thought, *Here it comes.* My lawyer was calling me to tell me that a trial date was set. When I got upstairs, I picked up the phone. My lawyer asked me if I was sitting down. I said no. He said, "Take a seat," and I did. He went on to say, "Ron, the man who said he saw you making a firebomb has come forth and admitted he lied and that he had perjured himself on the stand." He went on to say that since that was the only evidence they had against me, the Army was dropping all charges against me. I could not believe my ears. I had been held in confinement for almost a year, and just like that, I am free. Even though I was innocent, there were times when I thought that I would never see the light of day. With one phone call from my lawyer, I was free. He told me that the company was sending a driver to get me as we speak.

When I returned to my company, the general sent for me. This was the same general that would not meet with us that night and in whose office I was placed under arrest. What could he want with me? Maybe since he had time to think about it, he decided to bring the Afro products to the PX. (Well, at least my sense of humor is still intact.) This time when I got to his office, he asked me to take a seat. The general began by apologizing for the mistake the Army made. He went on to say that whatever he could do to help me get back to normal to let him know. Before I was summoned to the general's office, I had a meeting with my lawyer. He told me of the options I had. I had four months left on my tour of duty, but I could probably get an early out if I chose to. I did not hear the other options once I heard the early discharge. When the general asked if there was anything he could do for me, I said, "Sir, would you sign my discharge papers?" I believe he was more than happy to sign them. At this point, I was a disappointment to the Army or at least an embarrassment, and they wanted closure, and so did I. February 17, 1971, I was honorably discharged from the United States Army.

Spanish Harlem

After being discharged, I lived in Spanish Harlem for about four years. It was kind of strange because in Spanish Harlem, I was the foreigner. I got along well with the people basically because I attended to my own business, and I didn't run with a gang. I had two or three guys that I would hang out with but never with a gang. This was during the late sixties and early seventies when drugs flooded the streets of New York. It was as if they were airlifted and dropped into the area from airplanes. Drugs were everywhere, and you could get a bag of heroin for two dollars or three bags for five dollars.

There were four or five drug dealers in every block, mostly Spanish, in this part of the city. I was the only Black dealer in my block. As I said, because I tended to my own business, I did not get involved in too many hassles. Aside from having to go after a guy or two who I had credited some dope to who did not pay in a timely manner, I stayed clear of trouble. In this world, if an addict owes you money and did not pay, and you didn't go after him, then the word would go out and that would be bad for business, so even if you wanted to let it ride, you couldn't.

I remember there was this one guy (Puerto Rican) I gave drugs to on credit, and he didn't pay when he was supposed to. I had to go after him. He laid low for a few days, but since he was an addict, I knew sooner or later, he had to surface. I did not have to run around looking for him. I just had to wait for him to surface and be prepared to handle the situation when he did.

One night, I was walking down the street with my brother-in-law when I spotted this guy. He was standing up on the stoop with about five or six of his boys. I turned to my brother-in-law and told him to stand still about fifty feet from the stoop while I took care of business. I wanted them (the guys on the stoop) to think my brother-in-law had my back, which he did not, but more on him later. Anyway, I walked up to the stoop and started up, intentionally making eye contact with each man as I passed by. The guy I was after was at the top of the stoop, which meant I had to go by all his boys to reach him, and I did. I stopped about two feet in front of him and asked him, "Don't you owe me some money?" He said, "Yeah," and I asked, "Why I had not been paid?" He said, "I'm going to pay you," and as I looked him in the eye, I told him, "I know you are going to pay me, and I am going to tell you when!" (I am still looking him in the eye and purposely speaking loud enough for his boys to hear me. I was not yelling or screaming, just loud enough for all to hear.) I told him, "You have until noon tomorrow to pay, and if you did not, I am going to kick your head in. And then after I beat your butt, you will have another twenty-four hours to pay. If you don't, I am going to beat your butt again and again until you pay." I then turned and slowly walked down the steps, again making eye contact with each man as I did going up the stairs. I was paid the next day before noon.

As I have said, if an addict does not pay you, the word gets out, and when the business at hand is taken care of, that word gets out also. This is why I wanted all the guys on that stoop to hear me so they would get the word out. Instead of one guy spreading the word, I had six. The word went out fast that if you get credit from Ron, you better pay because he is crazy. This may sound crazy, but being thought of as crazy was good—who knew what a crazy person would do?

Doing things at high noon goes back to old west days. The reason they had gunfights at high noon was because everybody would be up and about. The whole town would be there, and the winner would get great publicity. The word would go out, "Don't mess with him because he gunned down Black Bart." After the incident on the stoop, my reputation spread throughout Spanish Harlem.

I wasn't using drugs. At the time, I saw it as a means of making money. I had teamed up with my mother's boyfriend (whom I called my stepfather) and my brother-in-law to sell drugs. Heroin was cheaper in the city than anywhere else in the tristate, and sold even cheaper in Harlem. So everybody was coming to Harlem for drugs, even the dealers. The heroin you bought in Harlem would sell for a higher price the further you took it out of Harlem. A two-dollar bag of heroin bought in Harlem would sell for five dollars in Brooklyn. If you crossed the Brooklyn Bridge, your profit would jump 150 percent. That same two-dollar bag sold for fifteen dollars in New Jersey and sold for twenty in Connecticut. We were thinking big. We would start in Brooklyn and eventually expand throughout the tristate.

Now as promised, more about my brother-in-law. Since he was born and raised in Brooklyn, he would be the main man there. He was on drugs, but either my reputation had not reached him or he thought it did not apply to him because he was with my sister. Anyway, we gave him five hundred bags to sell in Brooklyn and paid two guys to go with him to back him up. I woke up on the day he was supposed to leave, and he was gone. I went out on the stoop. I did not think anything of him being gone and figured he just got an early start. As I stood on the stoop looking around, I saw one of the guys that was to go with him. Then the alarm went off in my head. I asked him if he had seen my brother-in-law. He replied no and that he was waiting for him. I knew then something was up. Here, we had given him a package and were expecting him to return with five thousand dollars.

My sister was worried about what I was going to do to him. She had seen me go after people who owed me a lot less. I was hoping against hope that he would show up with the money, and all the worrying was for nothing, but with each passing day and no word from him, not even a call, my hope was dwindling and my anger increased. After a week, he finally called my sister and told her that he had been robbed and was afraid to face me. He told her that some guy robbed him with a razor. He was using my sister to make his appeal to me. I did not buy the story for a second. My mind told me that he went to Brooklyn and got up with his brother, a drug user also, and shot up my dope until it was gone. Then they cooked up the robbery story. I was not going to kill him, but I had planned on beating him but changed my mind because of my sister. I decided not to do either but to keep him on a very short lease. He and my sister lived with me, so I had to allow him to return home. I did this not for him but for my sister and my nephew.

My brother-in-law taught me a lesson that when it came to drugs, you could not trust anybody. In the drug game, there was one rule and that rule was there is no *rule*. Anything goes, and I do mean anything. In this world, you had to keep your eyes on everybody. You have to be on guard for the addict you did not take short money from or the addict you refused credit to, the stickup kids, the police, and even the guys who said, "Don't worry, Ron, I have your back." To those, I would say, they had my back, that makes two people that have my back. You just could not trust anybody.

After my brother-in-law did what he did to me, my stepfather and I put the idea of expanding on hold and decided to just concentrate on Spanish Harlem.

As I said, drugs in Harlem were the cheapest in the tristate area, and this brought people from all over to buy their drugs. Their problem was they did not have the right connections in Harlem. They could come and buy street drugs from the local dealer, but if they wanted weight, they had a problem. And if they were White, they really had a problem. Nobody trusted them. But still they came. They would give their money to a runner, hoping the runner would return with drugs. Nine times out of ten, the runner would not return, and the one time that he would come back, the runner would have tapped the bag (taking some out of the bag). But they would keep coming back even when the runner never returned. They still kept coming back.

There were a couple of White guys out of Connecticut who would come to Harlem to purchase drugs to take back and sell. I did not know at the time how much they were buying, but I knew they bought weight. They would come two or three times a week and pay this Puerto Rican to go to Harlem and get drugs for them. The Spanish guy they used to score for them was the kingpin of all the Spanish dealers in this area. I knew what was going on, but it was none of my business.

One night, I was approached by one of the White men and told that he and the Spanish kingpin had parted company. He asked if I could buy drugs for him. I had connections in Harlem (you have Spanish Harlem and Black Harlem. Fifth Avenue was the dividing line between the two), and the White guy knew it. I was excited about getting this man as a customer since it meant a lot of money. I did not entice this guy away from the Spanish in any way. He came to me, and I certainly was not going to turn this money away. I did not anticipate any trouble from the Spanish kingpin. After all, he knew me to be one to mind my own business.

I agreed to buy the drugs for the White guy from Connecticut. He told me he would be down two or three times a week depending on how fast he moved the dope back at home. He wanted to buy a thousand dollars' worth of heroin, and he would pay me two hundred each time he came. I began to do the math. I would make six hundred a week off the top, and in keeping with the tradition of tapping the package, a thousand dollars' worth meant he would actually get six hundred dollars' worth, but back in Connecticut, he would make between ten or twelve thousand dollars and did not lose. I found out that the Spanish kingpin was tapping the bag deeper than I was. The White guy told me that what I gave him for his money was a lot more than what the Spanish kingpin gave him. I was not trying to be too greedy. After all, I was getting paid three ways: First, I received two hundred up front. Second, my connection in Harlem gave me a bonus. Buying a thousand dollars' worth gave me about fifteen hundred dollars' worth. Third, I would tap in the White guy's bags. I had not started using the drugs, so I was making a lot of money. Everything was going really well, and then all hell broke loose. The Spanish kingpin saw I was getting bigger, and I guess he felt threatened. I knew he was jealous. When we crossed paths, there was a certain amount of tension. I knew he and his dealers had their eyes on my every move, and at the same time, I was not overly concerned because I had my eyes on their every move.

After a couple of months of doing business with the White guys, the Spanish kingpin approached me. I was coming out of my building to pick up drugs for the White guys when the kingpin approached me. He asked if we could talk. (This was the first time he had ever spoken to me beyond hey guy or what's up.) I said, "I am about to handle some business, but I've got a few minutes. What's up?" He knew what business I was talking about because the White guy was sitting in the car waiting for me. I did not want to hold him up for long. I really did not want him thinking I was plotting with the kingpin against him. Even though the White guy was satisfied with our arrangements, he was still paranoid. The White guys coming to Harlem for drugs were not stupid. They knew we were skimming from the bag, but as long as they made money, they were okay.

The kingpin got straight to the point. He said, "I don't want you to do anymore business with this Whitey." I felt kind of honored that he himself would come straight to me instead of sending one of his dealers with this message. After all, he had no less than fifty dealers and at least two hundred waiting to work for him, and any one of them would be only too happy to do his bidding.

I looked the kingpin in the eye and asked him, "What color was the White guy when he was doing business with you?"

He said, "He was green then."

"You want me to stop dealing with him because he is a 'Whitey' and I am a 'Brother'?" Then I told him, "If the 'Whitey' was green when you did business with him, he is also green to me."

With that, I was through talking, and I walked to the car. As I opened the passenger door and got in, the kingpin grabbed the handle, pulled the door open, and yelled, "I told you I don't want you to do business with this guy!"

As he pulled, let me tell you, if anyone tells you they got in a fight with one Puerto Rican, they are lying, and there were at least twelve of them. I pulled off my Lee jacket, tossed it to the ground, put my back to the car (making sure no one was behind me), and began swinging. Every blow I threw connected with one of them. It was kind of funny because they were hitting each other trying to hit me. I remember looking up on the stoop of my building to see my brother-in-law just standing there with his arm around my sister. I saw one of the guys coming at me with a cane, and I blocked it with my forearm and broke it. Then I heard one say, "I'm going to get my gun and shoot this nigger." I knew then it was time to go, and I managed to get in the car with the White guy. As soon as I closed the door, he pulled off. We had gone about three blocks when I thought about my Lee jacket, which I had tossed aside in the heat of the moment. It had dope and money in it.

I told the guy, "Stop the car. I have to go back."

He said, "If you go back now, they will kill you."

I said, "I still have to go back."

He stopped the car, and I got out and started to walk back.

As I slowly walked back, I was thinking how I would get back in the block without confrontation. I knew it was impossible and had no doubt that they would be waiting for me. I continued to walk slowly, and every sense I had was on high alert. As I approached my block, I saw two men talking in front of my building. I was too far away to make out who they were, and as I drew closer, I realized who they were—my stepfather and the Spanish kingpin. The kingpin was standing with one foot on the curb and the other on the sidewalk, talking to my stepfather. He was trying to explain to him what had happened. Once I saw my stepfather, I knew I had someone to watch my back, and I got mad all over again. I ran toward them and grabbed the kingpin by the collar of his full-length leather coat. Because of my momentum, I took him to the ground. I landed on top of him, reached for my knife, which was opened with a flick of my wrist. The kingpin saw the knife and began pleading for his life. As I began to bring my knife down, my stepfather grabbed my wrist, and at the same time, someone came from behind and hit me in the back of my head. My stepfather, who was built like Smoking Joe, hit the guy with a six-inch punch and laid him out cold. The guy was out cold on the street with his leg trembling.

My stepfather rushed me inside and into my apartment, but as we were going up the stoop, it looked like the whole Spanish nation was there, yelling threat after threat. I could not make out all that was said, but I did hear one say, "If you come back outside, you are a dead man." Once inside the safety of my apartment, I discovered my younger brother had picked up my jacket. Thinking back to the chaos, I remembered my brother, who was about twelve or thirteen at time, was there. I remembered hearing him screaming "Get off my brother!" and "Leave my brother alone!" while he was swinging a garbage can lid. I began to think about what had happened and the situation I was in. I thought about the threat "don't come back outside or we will kill you." I thought no one can tell me what to do and told my family I was going to the store. My family, my mother, stepfather, sister, and brother-in-law, pleaded with me not to go. As I listened, I remembered my brother-in-law standing on the stoop with his arm around my sister while I was fighting and decided to deal with him later. I was determined to show the Puerto Ricans that I was not afraid of them, so off I went to the store—alone. I was still pumped up from the fighting, and my adrenaline was high.

When I walked out on the stoop, it was really quiet. I walked toward the corner store more to show them up than to get anything and bought an apple. When I walked out, the kingpin came up on me and put a .38 special in my Afro. He said, "I ought to blow your brains out right here and now." I took a bite out of my apple and looked at him. I know he thought I was crazy. Here, I stood with a .38 aimed at my head, eating an apple. As I swallowed, I cleared my throat, looked him straight in the eyes, and saw that he was not going to shoot me. He said "I ought to blow your brains out," meaning he would not. I did not believe he had the heart to shoot me, and that was not his style. His MO was someone else would do his dirty work, and he had a number of guys who would have been happy to do it.

I asked him why he was going to shoot me. "Was it because I am out to make a dollar like you? When the White guy was dealing with you, that was fine, but when your arrangement went sour, and he came to me, that was not fine. He came to me, I did not go after him, and now you want to shoot me."

I took another bite of my apple, looked around at all of his boys standing there, and calmly walked away.

The next time I was standing on my stoop handling my business, I saw the kingpin and a couple of his boys approaching my stoop.

He walked up to me smiling and said, "I like the way you handle yourself, and I would like for you to come to work for me."

I looked at him and said, "I appreciate the offer, but no, thank you."

I explained that I worked alone and the reason I worked alone was if the money came up funny, I have only to answer to myself and not to him or anyone else. I never saw the White guy again. They probably found another connection, and I never had any trouble from the kingpin after that.

The Woman Behind the Man

———∽∽∽———

It is impossible to write this book without a chapter on my wife and daughters. There were a lot of people that put up with me when I was on drugs, but none of them did this 24-7 like my wife. Even though we are no longer together, she still plays a major part in my life. We have been in each other's lives for over thirty years and have three daughters and seven grandchildren. I thank God that I can still call her my friend, and she calls me friend especially now that I am able to look back. I can see my faults (which were many) and why our marriage did not work. I have told her that I do not blame her for leaving me. Believe me if I could have, I would have left me too. I know there were times during our marriage that she would look at me and think to herself, Lord, I have married a crazy man! I married a sure enough nut! But she stuck it out for as long as she could (twenty-two years), and when she could not take it anymore, she took the children and left.

When I met her, she was a young nineteen-year-old naive girl from Long Island, New York, and I was a young twenty-four-year-old hoodlum from Harlem. I guess you might say it was "the good girl bad guy attraction." When we met, she knew I was doing drugs, but she probably thought it was a phase I was going through. Little did she know that phase would last twenty-seven years. I still do not know how she put up with me for so long, and I will not attempt to. I will leave that to her. She may someday write her own book (I will be the first in line to purchase one) and tell her side of our story.

I do know that God blessed me by putting her in my life. There is no one on earth that knows me better. She has seen me at my worst, and hopefully, my best is yet to come. I have cried many a tear in this woman's arm with the exception of my mother and grandmother. There is no other man or woman that can say they have seen me cry. On one occasion, I was fired from a job two weeks before Christmas, and my first thought was to take this last check and go out and get drunk, but my second thought was this was my last paycheck before Christmas. I better take this money home to Net, and that was what I did. I remember crying while telling her I was fired and how hard it would be, if not impossible, to find work before Christmas. She put her arms around me and told me it would be all right.

I did not realize it then, but now I do. It was her love for me that kept me from going over the edge. Whenever I would get close to going over, she was there to pull me back. She usually would do it with a threat of leaving me, and I would attempt to straighten up. She did an excellent job of hiding my addiction from my daughters. There would be times when I would be under the influence, and my daughters would ask, "What is wrong with Daddy, Mama?" And my wife would say, "Leave your daddy alone. He is tired from working." Then she would send them out of the house to play. Then she would nudge me and tell me, "Go and lay across the bed. Your children are watching." I had the good sense to do what she told me. She never wanted the girls to think bad of their father.

Now I hate to think about just how many times I left the house to buy drugs, saying I would be right back. I did not realize that there was a good possibility that I might not be "right back." There was a good chance I could be picked up by the law, I could get robbed or, even worse, be killed, and she would never see me again. When I returned, she had a look of relief on her face that I was back safe. There would be times when I would ask her for money to get drugs, and because she could not bear the pressure of waiting for me to return, she said she would give me the money if I would take her with me. She did not get high, and I did not want to take her with me, but because my need to get high was so strong, I said okay. She would remain in the car while I went from dealer to dealer trying to purchase the best drug out there. All the while, my wife would sit there watching me. I guess she thought it was better sitting in the car than sitting at home worrying about me. I was so caught up in what I was doing (drugs) that I could not see her worry. I thought she was always nagging me. I did not realize she loved me. I could not have realized she loved me. I did not know what love was. Nobody ever taught me that. Back then, I would not have recognized love if it stepped up and slapped me in the face. But thank God, that was not the case now. I have learned how to love because God showed me how much he loved me (John 3:16). At the time, I loved my wife the best that I knew how. But through the teaching of Jesus Christ, I now love her in the way He has taught me, and that is a higher love.

As I said, my wife did not get high, did not drink, and did not smoke, and looking back, I had never been seriously involved with women who did. Some people say I was a picky, but I was not picky. I was greedy. I did not date women who did drugs because I did not want to share my dope. In my travels, I have met guys with wives or girlfriends who were hooked on drugs, and every time he got high, he would have to make sure he had enough for both of them. That was not for me. When I scored, it was mine, all mine! My wife was and still is a great mother. I remember watching her dress the girls, do their hair, and then get herself ready for work day after day. I was watching her one day going through her daily routine. I asked her, "How in the world are you able to do all you do and don't get high?" She said, "Because I don't have to get high," and that was her answer.

When I first met my wife, she took me to meet her family. It was my first visit to Long Island, and I saw for the first time Black people who had their own homes, cars, and boats. They actually had jobs and did not have to hustle to get them. I was greatly influenced by what I saw. I think it was around this time I began thinking about my future. I was working, but I wanted more. The job I had had a big layoff, and I was let go. My wife and I sat down, and we discussed me going to college. We agreed that she would work while I went to school, and after I graduated, she would go. We shook on it. I enrolled in college January 1979 with a major in accounting and minor in business administration. There is no doubt that her coming into my life changed me for the better. You will hear people say that drug addicts are dumb or stupid. I agree to the point that what we were doing was dumb and stupid, but the addict is far from dumb or stupid. I went to school three and a half years as a full-time student and graduated August 1982 with honors and a 3.6 GPA. I was elected student council president, held down a part-time job during the day, and get this, did heroin every day. Oh, did I fail to mention that I went back to school and graduated from college, and a tenth-grade education was all I had prior to enrolling in college? Yes, I was a high school dropout. I am taking this opportunity not to blow my own horn but to tell people that you too can do this, and I give credit to my wife, whom without her support I would have never achieved what I did.

I do not know if she felt it when I said to her I am sorry that I was not a better husband to her. The drug in which I was addicted would cause me to nod off as if I was asleep. It is strange how I thought I was nodding five or ten minutes, but in reality, it was closer to and twenty to thirty. Many times, when I came out of a trance and opened my eyes, she would be sitting there looking directly in my face.

What was you thinking sitting there? Did you need me for something? Did you want to talk to me about the girls or the house? In the twenty-two years, how many times did you need your husband, and I was not available? How many of those years, when you put them altogether, was I nodding off you? Forgive me. If I could, I would love to give you back each one of those years with flowers, but I cannot. Maybe when you write your book, you will answer these questions and maybe you will find it in your heart to forgive me. This might sound a bit strange, but you blessed me when you married me, and you blessed me when you left me. You blessed me coming and going.

I did not realize how excellent a job my wife had done in guarding my secret from my daughters until I got clean. She used to tell me, "Ron, your daughters are getting older, and it is time you sat them down and talk with them." But I would put it off. I did not realize that the pressure was getting to my wife. She was tired of the burden, and she wanted me to lift it from her.

One day, I was in withdrawal because I had not had my drugs for a couple of days. My daughter had been selling candy for the school. I asked her if I could borrow the money until I got paid. She said no because she had planned to turn the money in along with her friend early. I continued to plead with her to let me hold the money. After wearing her down, through tears in her eyes, she gave me the money. I left immediately to score. On the way, that little voice in my head told me, "Look at what you have done now." It said, "You actually made your daughter cry and took her money all so you could get high." I had to listen to that voice all the way to where I had to go to score. But that was all right because I knew how to shut that voice up. Once I got high, I would not hear it again. That night, a strange thing happened. I bought the dope and took it, but that voice did not shut up. I could still hear it talking. I have done many things to get high before, things that I am not proud of, but always, I was able to escape the guilt and shame once I got high, but not this time. This time, even though I got high, the guilt and shame of what I did to my child was still there. I knew then it was time to do something about my problem.

I decided it was time to talk to my daughters and tell them about my drug problem. I have done some difficult things in my life, but none could compare to what I had to do now. After telling them (my daughters) not to do drugs, I now have to confess to them that I was addicted to drugs. When I got home that night, I went straight to my bedroom. I was too guilt ridden to even look at my girls. I called my wife in first and told her my plan, and that plan was to finally talk with my children. After my wife left the room, I called in my daughters. I started with my oldest and worked my way to the youngest, who was nine. My oldest daughters were very understanding. They told me that they would support me in getting help with my problem, but next came my baby girl. I did not know how to tell her. After all, she was so young. I searched my mind trying to find a substitute word for drugs. Drugs is such a harsh word for a nine-year-old, but I could not find another word. She came into the room.

She noticed I was crying and asked, "Why are you crying, Daddy?"

I told her I had something to talk to her about. I said, "Baby, your daddy has a problem that he needs to get help with."

She asked, "What is the problem, Daddy?"

I just blurted it out. "I have a drug problem."

"Drugs!" she said. "You have been doing drugs? How long have you been doing drugs? You mean you have been doing drugs? Where are you getting these drugs?"

These questions took me totally by surprise. "Whoa, baby, whoa, I cannot answer all your questions now. I just wanted to tell you that I have a problem, and I will be seeking help with it."

I knew that after having that talk with the girls, I had to seek help. The next day, I packed my clothes. I did not know where I was going, but I knew I had to leave home. I knew I had to make things better. I had to change.

I left that day with my duffel bag on my shoulder and suitcase in hand. I have never felt so empty in my life. I did not stop getting high, but after that night with my daughter and telling them about my problem, getting high was never the same. I could not get away from that voice of guilt and shame. I was lost and facing the reality that the one thing I wanted to be good at I was failing. I wanted to be a good father. Just like when I was a child, it was back to the street, sleeping wherever I laid my head, eating from the garbage can, and being reduced to the animalistic level. All I wanted to do was get high enough to make the voice shut up!

I could not hold down a job. I would work odd jobs and would always quit for one reason or another. The real reason was drugs. I could not work without them and did not want to work when I had them. When I did not have drugs, I was in physical pain, and when I was high, I did not want to work because working would blow my high. Drugs had taken over. I could not sleep without them, and I enjoyed the high too much to sleep. Everything took second place to the drugs: eating, sleeping, working, friends, and family. I could be sitting at a table covered with drugs, my physical body would be sitting there doing the drug, but my mind would be on the prowl for more. No matter how much I had in my possession, it was never enough. I was stuck in the mental state of where is the next hit coming from. It is strange how I turned to drugs to escape all bad things that had happened to me as a child, and now I was doing drugs to escape all the terrible things I had done. I was trapped. I remember having a pocket full of dope and money, crying to the Lord to help me. I do not want to do this anymore, but I cannot stop. I need your help, Lord!

At this point, I had never been to jail except for the eight months I spent in the stockades in Europe. I had no criminal record. This was a miracle because I had done things that could have landed me in jail. But by being out on the street, my luck ran out. One night, a friend of mine told me about a tractor trailer that was loaded with custom rims. He said it was parked in the back of an auto shop. The friend told me that it was parked there for the weekend, and they would probably unload it on Monday. Since it was Saturday night, I was going to do the job. I had two days to do it in. One of the reasons I had not been to jail was because whenever I did anything, I did it by myself. The less people involved, the better my chances of getting away. I pretended I was not interested, but I had planned to do it that night by myself. I drove out to the site and looked around until I spotted the trailer. The back of the store was dark. There were lights in the front and on the sides, but none in the back. It was perfect.

I parked my car a couple of blocks away and walked back to the trailer. The trailer had a steel band that locked the doors. I was shocked to find there was no lock on it. After cutting the band, I opened the door, went inside, and closed the door behind me. I turned on the flashlight, and there they were, just like the guy said, custom rims. Now I had to figure out how to move them all in two days by myself. I began thinking and went back outside to have a look. There was a heavy wooded area about fifty yards from the trailer. I decided to move the rims and store them in the woods. I worked for the next two days moving the rims. As soon as night fell, I went to work. By late Sunday night, I had them all moved and hidden in the trees and bushes. As I took orders, I could go to the site at night to get them. It was all going according to my plan until I ran out of sales. I had sold about half the rims before the sales dropped.

I was getting desperate. I was not selling the rims, and my addiction was full blown. Since the rims were made of solid aluminum, I started selling them to the local scrapyard. I would take them out of the box, bend them up a little, and sell them for scrap aluminum. I could not move them quick enough in my car, so I decided to get someone with a truck to help me. That was my big mistake. There was a guy I knew that had a truck, and he would take girls to shoplift for a share of what they stole. I figured he would be interested in my offer. I told him my plan and that I would give him thirty dollars on every hundred and that all he would be doing was the driving. I would load the truck. All he had to do was transport the stuff. I was sure it was a better deal than he was getting with the ladies, and he accepted my offer. Between selling the rims to the scrapyards and the few sales we made to people, I was doing five hundred to a thousand dollars a day. Everything was going well. I was able to get high enough to quiet the voices. I would get so high that I would pass out.

I did not write this book out of guilt or shame because I have repented for my sins, God has forgiven me of them, and he has taught me how to forgive myself. You see, that was my problem all along, not God's forgiveness for that he freely gives to whoever asks, but I could not forgive myself. God not only forgave me, but through his grace, he has removed the burden of guilt and shame. God knows that I would not be able to write this book if I was still carrying around the guilt of what I had done. God freed me to tell my story. It is through that same mercy and grace that I write. I want to tell somebody who is suffering that the same grace that God has extended to me God will give to you.

As with all good things (worldly good things), they come to an end. There were no more customers for the rims, and we were now selling them to the scrapyard for junk. One day, we took a load to the yard, and usually, when we took them, we would be in and out, no questions asked. But this time, there seemed to be a hold up. The people at the yard were hesitating in paying me. They were making excuses. First, they wanted to check the weight of the load, and then they wanted to be sure that it was all aluminum. All of this was out of the ordinary. I knew something was wrong, but I was ill from not having my dope, and I dismissed that thought. Finally, the man gave the cashier the all-clear sign to pay me. I thought to myself, *See, you were paranoid over nothing.* As we walked out of the office, a man followed us, and I noticed the name on his work shirt. It was the name of the auto store that the rims had come from. The store had alerted all the scrapyards in the area to be on the lookout for anyone that brought in any aluminum rims. The man from the auto store asked if he could speak with us. I said no but that if he gave me his card, I would call him. I had the money now and was in a hurry to get out of there. The man went back into the office, and I turned to my partner and said, "Let's get out of here." He said no. He was not going anywhere because he did not want to lose his truck. I said, "They already had the truck's plate number, so we might as well make a run for it," but he refused to move the truck. I noticed that he was freezing up on me, and he was scared.

I had to think and think fast. The first thing I had to do was calm my partner down so he would not say or do anything stupid. I knew the police were on the way, so I did not have much time. I came up with a story, a lie, that we would tell the police when they came. We would tell them that we were out looking for junk metal when we ran across the rims. That way, all they can charge us with is possession of stolen property instead of charging us with burglary and larceny. "Okay?" I asked. My partner said no that they were going to want to know more than that. I knew then I was in trouble. When we were making all that money, I was the man. Now I was on my own. I continued to try to convince him that my plan would work, but to no avail. He had his own plan, and that was to tell on me.

He could not wait, and he ran for the police so fast that you would have thought they was holding him hostage. I mean he was even crying real tears, telling the police that it was all me. Even the police asked me how in the world I hooked up with this guy. This guy talking so fast, he answered questions that the police had not even asked. He got on their nerves, and they told him unless I collaborated his story that we both would be charged with burglary and grand larceny. Then this guy turned to me and began pleading with me to confess. He better thank God I had handcuffs on because if I had not, I would have been charged with an assault charge too. They took us to jail and charged us both with burglary and grand larceny. They gave us a bail, but I did not have anyone to call. The other guy's mama came and bailed him out.

I stayed in jail for four months, and during that time, I had the time to think about my life. I did not know how, but I knew that I was going to turn things around, or I would die out there. My thoughts turned to my daughters. I knew my marriage was over, but I had to consider them. I did not want to die a junkie, and I wanted my daughters to be proud to call me Daddy. I have not done much lately to make them proud of me, and now I was in jail. I decided to own up to the crime and throw myself at the mercy of the court. This was my first charge, and I figured as a first offender, the judge would probably give me probation. I got in touch with my legal aid lawyer and told him my plan. When we got to court, I pleaded guilty of all charges. The judge gave me two years' probation and released me. When I got out, I had no place to go. I did not want to see my daughters. I did not want to see them until I had gotten the help I told them I was leaving to get.

I ended up on the doorstep of a friend. She had six children and lived in one of the projects. I told her of my situation and that I had no place to go and was not working, and she took me in. I found a job soon after moving in and was able to give her something for letting me stay there. I worked a couple of months without using drugs. I was operating on sheer willpower. But that did not last, and it was not long before I was back to using drugs. I could not stop. This time, I just gave up and thought I am going to die a drug addict. I was unaware that God had other ideas for me.

Signs of Recovery

—◦◦◦◦—

If you relapse before you actually pick up the drug, then your recovery starts before you actually put down the drug. There were a series of incidents that happened that led to my seeking recovery. In the past, I have tried every way I knew how to stop using on my own. I swore on my marriage, my children, my jobs, and my mother's grave and even went to jail and swore that was it, only to start using again. Some of my most sincere prayers were prayed while I had drugs in my pocket, yet I begged God to help. I did not think God heard me because I still got high. I did not know. I thought once you asked God to help you and that if he really cared, he would help me right then and there. But since I used right after the prayer, I guess God was not listening to me.

There were things I was doing to get high that I did not like, and it was these things that led me to pray. As addicts, there were things that we said we would never do to get high, and then there was a list of things we said we would never ever, ever do. That was when the signals go on that say you are really in trouble. I had begun to do these things. One day, I was sitting around with no money and wanted to get high. My wife had gone shopping for the girls, and she always kept the receipts. I decided to sneak the clothes out of the house, take them back to the store, and use the money to get high on. I told myself I would replace the clothes when I got paid. I had made a solemn vow not to steal from my children for drugs, and I began to break that vow.

There was another time when I actually contemplated killing a man for drugs. You see, there was this man in the neighborhood who

64

kept a large amount of cash on him at all times. Since he knew me, I knew I could not just walk up to him and say this is a stickup. He could identify me. So I was left with no other alternative but to hurt him or kill him. Even though I never did it, I was bothered by the thought that I would even think about killing someone just to get high for no other reason—not to feed my family or buy shoes for my children—but so I could buy dope. I knew I was in trouble. Then there was the time my daughter cried and begged me not to take her money, but I convinced her that I would put it back. A strange thing happened to me that night when I went to score. I was standing in line waiting my turn to be served when the dealer looked beyond the people in front of me and asked, "How many bags you want, Pops?" I looked behind me to see who he was talking to, to see who he was calling Pops. The dealer looked at me and said, "I am talking to you, Pops." I said, "Give me three bags."

When I left that hallway, the dealer's words still rang in my ears, "How many do you want, Pops?" It was as if he had slapped me in the face with reality. "Pops." I was a Pops. I looked into the mirror, the mirror of my soul, and staring back at me was Pops, and I began to cry. I cried because it was not my plan to stay out there that long. When I started, it was only supposed to be just one weekend. This was in the summer of '71, and now it was the summer of '98, and I was Pops. I had gone from being a nineteen-year-old teenager to a "Pops." Where did all that time go? I now refer to that time as the "Rip Van Winkle" syndrome. Mr. Winkle slept twenty years, and I had slept twenty-seven.

The Good Samaritan

Luke 10:30–37

For twenty-seven years, I was addicted to a drug called heroin. All that time, I was able to give myself an excuse to use. For twenty-seven years that comes to 9,855 days, I had a reason to get high. From my own experience and listening to the experience of other former addicts, I am convinced that because of events that occurred doing our childhood, our formative years, we were set up to be addicted. The event for me was my father leaving practically the day I was born. Then there was my mother and her alcohol addiction. She married a very abusive man, who abused her and me. He too was also alcohol addicted.

To say I had low self-esteem would be the understatement of the century. After all I went through at home, I had to go outside and make believe everything was all right. I had to pretend I was normal. There is no wonder heroin and I became such good friends. When I got high, it did not matter, nothing mattered! The only thing that eventually mattered was that I did not run out of heroin. As long as I had heroin, everything would work out.

I started out blaming my father, mother, and stepfather. Then the blame spread to everybody who had authority over me. Then I blamed my wife, my children, my friends, my boss, the weather, the dog, the cat, and, when I could not find anything to blame, on anybody. I always had my favorite whipping boy, "the White man." Every Black person could relate to the White man holding me back. My excuses became so ridiculous. I started blaming the dope dealer.

My reasoning was if the dope dealer did not sell dope, I could not buy it. Then I blamed the police figuring if they did their job and locked up all the dope dealers, I could not buy any. I blamed everyone but me. My problem was everybody's fault but mine. I even blame the Afghans for growing the stuff. You see, I was an innocent victim tiptoeing through the tulips, and everybody was messing with me. I called it "the Charlie Brown syndrome." Why is everybody always picking on me?

After twenty-seven years of drug abuse, on August 20, 1998, I woke up and placed my feet on the floor, still sitting on the bed. I began contemplating how I was going to get high today. This had been my thoughts every morning for almost three decades. How am I going to get my drugs? Who can I manipulate? Who can I lie to? Who can I steal from? These were my thoughts. Little did I know that I was not going to get high this day or the next day or the next. Little did I know I would not be getting high anymore!

It is kind of strange when I write about it in retrospect. I mean I did not plan to stop on this specific day. I did not go to bed the night before, thinking tomorrow I would stop getting high. As I was sitting on the side of the bed contemplating how I would get high, my thoughts were interrupted by this feeling of tiredness. I do not mean being tired as if I needed sleep since I had just woken up. I mean tired of life, tired of living this way, and tired of drugs and the things I would do to get them and trying to justify my actions with insane reasoning.

There was a certain lawyer who put the question to Jesus, "Who is my neighbor?" If you read the Bible as you would read any other book, you would get little or nothing from it. You would be left wondering why you don't get it. Until you can read it and relate it to you or your experiences, it is just another book. But when you read it and see yourself, then you can relate, and the word becomes alive in you, this is what is meant by the phrase "the living word."

August 20, 1998, I sat on the edge of that urine-stained mattress. The room itself had a heavy smell of urine because the child who slept in the bed was a bed wetter. I was homeless, and the child's mother had taken me in. Since I did not have any other place to sleep, I could not complain. I sat there as my life flashed before my eyes. During the height of the famine in Africa, I spoke at the UN, I graduated from college, and I was elected president of the local chapter of the urban league, director of the youth summer program, married, and the father of five girls, and here I sat on a urine-stained mattress. Thoughts of killing myself filled my head, and the idea had a real appeal to me. Thoughts of how I had made a mess of my life and how I had failed all who cared about me, this made suicide even more appealing. Twenty-seven years of substance (heroin) abuse had taken its toll on my life.

One year prior to this day, I met a man named Ken, whom I had confided in about my drug problem. Looking back, I believe the process of recovery starts before you actually stop using drugs. When I admitted using drugs to Ken, my process had begun. I did not realize it at the time though. Ken gave me his card and told me if I ever got serious about getting help with my problem to call him, but if I am not ready, don't bother to calling him. I took the card, put that card in my back pocket, and carried it for about a year. Periodically, I would look at it when things got rough, think about calling, and never did. I eventually lost his card. On the day I sat there on that bed with thoughts of taking my life, in the midst of my confusing thoughts, God sent me one simple message, and that was to call the number, and Ken's number appeared to me. I had not realized that during those times when I would take that card out of my pocket and contemplated calling it, I had memorized the number, and now God brought it to my mind at the moment I needed it most.

I was in deep withdrawal from heroin, dry mouth, backaches, legs cramping, and diarrhea. I made my way from that room and down the steps to the phone. I dialed the number, a man answered, I asked for Ken, and moments later, Ken answered. All I could say was I needed help. He asked where I was, and I gave him the address. Ken said to not worry, and he would be there soon. I hung up the phone and made my way back upstairs to that urine-stained room.

I had always considered myself as a true survivor that no matter what happened, I would survive. I had a saying on the street that I was known for, and it was "I don't care if the mule goes blind. I have to have mine!" I got this saying from my grandfather. He was a farmer, and the saying meant "even if the mule goes blind, he still had to get the field plowed." And when I said it, it meant no matter what happened, I had to have my heroin! This became my battle cry. Another saying my grandfather had was "If a mosquito can pull a plow, do not ask how. Just hook him up." Like I said, I am a survivor. I always had an ace up my sleeve and a trick in my bag, or I could pull a rabbit out of my hat. But I was at the end of my rope. There was no aces up my sleeve, no tricks left in my bag, and no rabbit left to pull out of my hat. All the excuses I had given myself to use drugs over twenty-seven years were crashing down around me. It was like the house of cards tumbling in. The enormous weight of all those years fell on my shoulders, and I became so tired, so very tired. I wasn't tired where I needed a good night rest. I had the kind of tiredness that only death could give me. That was the kind of rest I was looking for. It is kind of ironic that I would write this book from this room in the midst of the smell of urine in the air. I mean ironic because in my mind, that is what I had done with my life, urined it away.

I heard Ken's voice downstairs, talking to the young lady of the house. He asked for me, and I heard her direct him upstairs to the room I was in. I had called Ken at eleven o'clock. It was now twelve noon, and he was here. As I sat waiting for him to come into the room, I was feeling embarrassed by the room and the state that I was in. My pride was rearing its ugly head. My pride had me eating out of garbage cans and sleeping in abandoned cars, under houses, and abandoned buildings, and I was too proud to ask anyone for help. I remember going into an abandoned building and sleeping in the closet. I slept with my feet pressed against the door so if anyone tried to get in, they would wake me. (Proverb 16:18 says, "Pride goes before destruction." Proverb 18:12 says, "Before destruction the heart of a man is haughty and before honor is humility.") Ken entered the room despite the heavy stench of urine, and he did not hold his nose or frown. He asked me, "Where are your clothes? Are you ready to go?" I pointed to a pile of dirty clothes in the corner, and this White man began to fold these dirty clothes with such care.

You would think he was taking them from a dryer. Then he turned to me and asked me again if I was ready. I said yes. At this point, I did not have any idea where I was going, but I trusted Ken. I believed he was going to help me. I was so weak from withdrawal that I could not make it downstairs without help. This White man picked up my duffel bag with one hand and with the other hand around my waist, assisting me down the stairs.

I mention Ken's race because it was sort of a revelation in it for me. I talked about the many excuses I used to justify and rationalize my continual drug use. Well, as a Black man, I made the White man my whipping boy. Whenever I could not blame anyone else for my life's failures, I could always blame the White man. Here I was, my life literally being saved by who? A White man! I can't imagine what would have happened if Ken had not answered the phone that day.

As we rode, Ken told me he had been in touch with a detox center, and that was where we were heading. I was so depressed that I did not think anything or anyone could help me. I was willing to try. Ken saw the state I was in and tried to assure me that everything would be all right. Trust in God, and he will see you through. I did not believe God would even listen to me anymore. He had helped me so many times before only to have me go back to drugs again and again. Why would God listen to my prayer? But Ken assured me God will see me through.

We arrived at the detox center and went inside. Ken did the talking, asking if they had a bed. The nurse said there was a bed available, but in order for me to be admitted without paying, I had to be a resident of that city. Since I was not a resident, I had to pay. My heart dropped, but Ken took out his checkbook and wrote a check for my entire treatment. Then we went out for dinner. Ken bought me a Bible and gave me fifty dollars for shaving gel, soap, deodorant, etc. We headed back to the center. Ken prayed for me. He told me not to worry because God was going to raise me from this day. When we got back to the detox center, Ken gave the nurse his card and told her if I needed anything to call him.

I told Ken I would repay him. He said I didn't owe him anything but that God was going to raise me from today and that I gave back what was so freely given to me today. Then he left, and I had not seen Ken since that day.

After Ken left, the nurse showed me to my room. I just wanted to be alone and not bothered by anyone. She offered to give me Tylenol, but I said no. After all, drugs were what got me here. When the nurse left, and the door closed, I got what I wanted—to be left alone. As I surveyed the room, I found there was one window that allowed the sun to shine brightly through. My first thought was to get rid of all that light. I craved the darkness. Joel 3:15 says, "The sun and the moon was darkened, and the stars shall withdraw their shining." This is the kind of darkness I craved. There were some old army blankets in the closet. I took one out and covered the window. This put the whole room in total darkness. I lay down on the bed. The pains of withdrawal were intensifying. I remember seeking medical help, and the doctor offered me a drug called methadone. I was seeking help for my drug problem, and the doctor offered to help me with drugs. I told the doctor I did not want any other drugs. Then the doctor said the two words that no addict wants to hear. He said, "Then your only other alternative is 'cold turkey.'" As I lay on the bed in pitch darkness, those words echoed through my head, cold turkey, cold turkey.

My legs were cramping so bad that I drew up in the fetus position. (John 3:4–6 says, "Nicodemus says unto Jesus how can a man be born again when he is old? Can he enter the second time into his mother's womb and be born again? Jesus answered, truly, truly I say unto thee; except a man is born of water and of the Spirit he cannot enter into the Kingdom of God. That which is born unto the flesh is flesh and that which is born of the Spirit is Spirit.") As I lay there in the fetal position, my spiritual birth was taking place. I stayed in the fetal position for three days.

I met an old man during my youth. He saw me partying and chasing women and called me over to him. He asked me if I was having a good time and enjoying life.

I said, "Yes, I am."

He said, "Good, but the day will come when you will have to pay for all this fun that you are having. One day, you will have to pay the piper."

I did not understand truly what that old man was saying until now. Now I will have to pay for all that fun. The door opened and flooded the room with light. It was the nurse checking on me. I screamed and yelled for her to get out and close the door. I thank God for the training she had. She did not react to me. She simply closed the door and left. I later apologized to her. I just wanted to be left alone in the darkness.

I had never experienced anything like this before. My throat seemed to have a lump the size of an egg in it. No matter how much I swallowed, it would not go down. My entire back ached. I had thrown up until there was nothing to throw up. Then I started with the dry heaves. My stomach cramped along with diarrhea. I had resigned myself to the fact that I would never ever to sleep again. I would lie there praying for sleep and fall asleep only to wake up wide-eyed five minutes later. I would sleep for five or ten minutes and stay awake for two or three hours. I would get up and wring sweat off my sheets from cold sweating. There was a mirror in the room, and when I looked in it, I did not recognize myself. I remember saying out loud, "This person in the mirror is not me." I did not know who it was, but I knew it was not me.

Coming out of the world of drugs, I had a serious trust issue. I mean I did not trust anybody. God knew this, but he encouraged me to trust the people that he would be sending into my life. At this point, I wanted help. I needed help. I wanted to stop using drugs, but I could not do it alone. I did not know how to stop. This brings me to my sessions with the hypnotherapist. They say there are two types of people that cannot be hypnotized. One is a very smart person, and the other is a very stupid person. In order to hypnotize a person, the subject must be able to center his thoughts, able to focus. Well, a smart person can scatter his thoughts, and a person who is not smart, his thoughts are always scattered. I do not know how I fit in. All I knew was I needed help and was willing to try anything that they said would help me.

I walked into the therapist's office. She asked me to take a seat. At this point, I had maybe four days clean of drugs after twenty-seven years of continual use. I was full of fear, and I was very nervous as

I sat down. She began telling me about the procedure. She told me that I would not be under full hypnosis but semihypnosis and that I would be aware of everything around me and that at any point I felt uncomfortable and did not want to continue, I could stop this session. I was very relieved at hearing this. I have always been afraid of losing control, and when she told me I had the power to stop the procedure whenever I chose, I felt a sense of control. So I trusted her and said, "Okay, let's do it."

She got up and led me into an inner room adjacent to her office. I guess she sensed my nervousness. She told me to relax. I looked around the room. On the wall, she had a screen projecting a film of the ocean and waves rolling up against the shoreline and what looked to be a thousand swans with their wings spread. It looked as if they were dancing to the rhythm of the waves. Just looking at the pictures, I began to relax. There was a sound of chimes twinkling as if the wind was coming off the ocean and blowing gently through the chimes. I relaxed even more.

The therapist had a leather recliner in the room along with a leather armchair. She sat down in the armchair, and I sat in the recliner. She instructed me to go ahead and recline the chair. As I reclined, I remember thinking, *This must be the point where she takes out the watch with the chain on it, swing it back and forth, and then says your eyes are getting heavy*. I guess I had watched too many Alfred Hitchcock movies, but that did not happen.

Her chair was right next to the recliner. She took my hand and began telling me to relax.

"First, relax your breathing. Inhale, exhale, inhale, exhale." Slowly, she said, "Inhale, exhale."

I began to slow my breathing. Then she told me to let my mind relax.

"Now relax your neck, your shoulders, your arms, your hands."

She let go of my hand, and she moved on down to my feet. I was in a state of total relaxation. I was relaxed like I have never been before, and I was calm. I put my total trust in that voice that was so calm, so gentle, and so soft. She asked if I was relaxed, and I said I was.

The therapist then asked me to go back.

"Go back to the last time you remember your whole family was together. I want you to go back to the house where you last lived with your whole family, your mother, stepfather, sisters, and brothers."

She asked if I could see the house.

"Yes, I can see it," I answered.

She then asked me to describe the house. She said, "Don't go inside yet. I just want you to describe the scene."

I said it was evening. There was a large clock across the street that said five o'clock in the afternoon. I described the house. It was a two-story, white with green trim, with a swing on the porch. After describing everything I saw, the therapist told me to go up the steps and into the house and tell her what I saw, and I did. I walked up the steps and into the front door. There standing in the living room was my mother, stepfather, and their friends drinking and having a good time. I stood there watching. Then the scene changed. My mother told my stepfather she was going out tonight. This usually set my stepfather off because when my mother tells him she is going out, she means by herself, and this started an argument that nine out of ten times led to a fight. Their arguing got louder and louder.

I heard the therapist's voice telling me to go to the part of the house I would go to when they argued. I walked past my parents and went upstairs. There were three bedrooms upstairs. I went to the door of the room I shared with my brothers. I turned the knob, opened the door, and went in. There sitting on the bed was me, little Ronnie. All my sisters and brothers were around me. As far as I could, I had my arms stretched out in an effort to embrace them all and tell them not to cry that everything would be all right. Then a strange thing happened. All this time, no one was aware of my presence. As little Ronnie was comforting his siblings, he looked directly into my eyes. He needed somebody to put their arms around him and tell him everything would be all right. I began to cry, and I went to little Ronnie, put my arms around him, held him tight, and told him that it would be all right.

The therapist told me it was time to leave. Her voice sounded so far away. Before, it sounded like it was right in my ear, but now it seemed far off. I remember saying, "I don't want to leave him [little Ronnie]. Everybody always leaves him, and I wanted to stay with him." The therapist told me to tell little Ronnie I have to leave. I told little Ronnie I loved him and would protect him from now on. The therapist's voice was closer now.

"Ron, Ron, it's time to leave," and I came back. When I came to the front of my shirt was wet with tears. I was crying but relieved at the same time. I had met myself, an experience I will always be thankful for and never will forget.

The Truth Revealed

What Will People Say?

For as many people past, present, and future, there is a story to be told. My story is one out of billions. There are many reasons why people do not tell their stories. Fear however is really the only reason. Fear is the seed that was planted in us early on, and all other reasons are the manifestations of that seed—the fear of what people will say, the fear of who they will hurt, and the fear of having to face the real truth about oneself while putting it down on paper. The reason I know this is because I have suffered these same fears. Not only did I suffer these fears, but as a minister of the Gospel, I have had countless conversations with people who suffered these fears too.

As God has given gifts to all of us, and some of us are multi-gifted, God has given me many gifts, and one of these gifts is to disarm people. When you meet a stranger, your defenses go up. You are wondering what he wants or what is he after. As I speak with people, they soon realize I am not after anything, and it is safe to talk with me. People have things going on in their lives and need someone to talk to, someone that will really listen to them. As a minister, you would probably think I would meet these people in the church, but this is not the case. I find that a vast majority of the "church folk" live in a pretend world. The people I am talking about, the strangers who confide in me some of their darkest secrets, I meet them on the bus, supermarket aisles, checkout counters (many have paid for my groceries), Laundromats, ball games, picnics, and just about any place that people go. It seems like I am meeting these people everywhere but in church.

Fear is the only thing that stands between us and true happiness, true peace, true love, and true success. If we don't face up to our fear, it will accompany us to our grave.

I had an uncle (my mother's brother) who was dying from cancer. He called me from the hospital to tell me he did not want to die in the hospital and asked if I would come and get him. I said yes and took him home with me and my family. One night we were sitting up late talking, he could not sleep because he was busy dying. I would sit and listen to him talk and talk. He told me that he wanted to go to church, but he was afraid of what the church folk would say about him.

He said, "They would probably say stuff like I did not come to church in my life, and now that I am dying, I have the nerve to come to church."

I really wanted to say to my dying uncle that this was not true and that the church folk would welcome him. They would love and comfort him in his time of need. But the real truth was there would be some who would say exactly what he said they would say. This was Monday night and my uncle died that Wednesday. He had two days left on earth and wanted to go to church but was afraid of what would be said about him. I told him that Monday night that he did not have to go to church to make his peace and that he could do it right here. The next day, my uncle called me to his bedside. He told me, when he passed, "Do not let anyone take me into a church," but if I wanted to say a few things at his grave site, that was okay. I believe my uncle made his peace with God, and I honored his last wish.

Even though we want to tell somebody what we are going through, but who will truly understand? In my travels, I met a lady. She lady who was in her late sixties, and she confessed to me that she had an alcohol problem. This lady was looking for someone who would listen and understand her plight. She chose me. What I know is whenever there is an alcohol problem or drug problem, there are deeper problems. There are underlying issues that lead us to drink and do drugs, and unless these problems are exposed, there will be no recovery. This lady was ready to expose the very thing that drove her to drink. This was a sign that she was getting tired of the things that drinking made her do. She did not like the person the drinking had turned her into. It is not just a matter what drinking caused her to do but a matter of what caused her to drink.

Her confession was that at the age of sixteen, she became pregnant, and the boy abandoned her. During this period (the fifties) when a girl got pregnant out of wedlock, she was looked down on in shame. During this time, not only was the girl looked at with shame, but she bought that same shame on her family. A lot of families would send the child off, away from home to stay with relatives in another state. Now this woman told me how she tried to hide her condition from the family until she could get an abortion. Since abortions were illegal at the time, she went in search of what was called at the time a back-alley abortion. She told me how she ran across a lady who would perform it for fifty dollars. Fifty dollars she did not have. She went to the boy, and that was when he disappeared. The young girl, sixteen years old, was left alone in her predicament. She was in such a state of desperation, so desperate that she decided to give herself the abortion.

This woman was crying. Here she was in her late sixties weeping for that sixteen-year-old girl and her baby, and I was crying with her. She went on to tell me how she went into that bathroom alone and did the deed. She told how she sat there with the fetus in her hands in total shock. Then she told me how she could not look at her hands anymore without seeing that baby. The only time she could forget was when she was drunk. Now we were getting down to the real nitty-gritty, the root of her issue. Her problem was not drinking. Her problem was that abortion.

I thank God I was placed there to tell her that God will forgive her. You see, some of us have done such horrible things that we think there is no way we can be forgiven. When we think this way, we only sink deeper into our sins. But it is not that God will not forgive us. It is that we will not forgive ourselves. God brings us to the root of our problems, such as he did with this woman and with me. For years, we did things and did not know why we did them. I would like to be able to tell you that there are other ways of getting out of the mess we get ourselves into, but I cannot. God is the only way. Through his son, Jesus Christ, we can be made free.

Unfamiliar Land

—❦—

In Genesis chapter 12 verse 1, God told Abram (who later was called Abraham) to get thee out of thy country. When I finished the detox treatment, I was left with nowhere to go. The day before I left, I was depressed. The drugs were out of my system, but what do I do now, and where will I go? I knew I did not want to go back where I had come from. There was nothing there except what I had just gotten rid of, drugs. I was sitting around when I overheard about a residential drug rehabilitation program offered by the Veteran Affairs Medical Center. I inquired about the program and was told by the nurse that she would call and see if I was eligible for the program. She did, and I was told I qualified for the program. An appointment was made for me on the next day. I felt a little hope return to me. I was determined not to go back where I came from and that I would make the best of this opportunity if given the chance.

I arrived at the VA Hospital the next day not knowing what to expect. I checked into the clinic, and they immediately began a battery of test as part of the intake process. At any point during these tests, you could be dropped from the program, and that made me so nervous. I really wanted this chance. I remember being in a thirty-day clinic and praying, asking God to please give me another chance.

"I confess, Lord, that I messed up, but I promise, Lord, if you give me another chance, I will get it right."

I saw the VA Hospital as my one last chance to get it together. I passed all the tests and was cleared to go on to the final test, and if I pass this one, I am in. The last test was an interview before a panel of four counselors who question you about your drug history. They really wanted to see if you were sincere in your desire to change your life. Outside the interview room was a couch where potential clients would sit, waiting to be called. I sat there with my head hung low and wondering, *If they turn me down, where will I go? What will I do?*

I looked around, and there were people everywhere coming and going in all directions, and they all seemed to have a purpose. I never felt so alone or so out of it all. Finally, my name was called, and I was led into a room with a long table and chairs on each side, and I took a seat. There were four counselors, and they each began to question me individually. How long have you been on drugs? Have you ever sought help before? What makes you think you are ready to change? I answered all their questions, and when they asked me, "What makes you think you are ready?" I just said because I am so tired. When I said that, they gave me a look that said we believe you are. Then they said the words I had been waiting for ever since I got here.

"Mr. Warren, we are going to give you an opportunity to change your life."

I said thank you. It felt like a building was lifted off my shoulders. I remember thanking God and promising him that I would make the best of this chance.

The therapy was very intense. I was given a sheet of paper with meetings and times I was supposed to be there along with classes. Every hour of every day, I had to be accounted for. I could not leave the VA grounds for the first six weeks. That did not bother me because I did not have anyplace to go. I was a total stranger in this land, and I did not know anybody. All I had was God. But there was one class that kind of stood out. It was spirituality. This class was taught by a Roman Catholic priest by the name of Father Lloyd Stephenson. This class was scheduled in two weeks, and I did not know what to expect from it, but like I said, I was willing to try anything.

For the whole two weeks, I kept hearing about this man, Father Stephenson and the spirituality class. I would see people coming out after the class let out, and they were laughing and talking about the things that went on in class. This helped to fuel my curiosity. Over the next two weeks, I began to look forward to it. I would notice that no one carried a Bible, and nobody came out of the class quoting scripture. What kind of spirituality class was this with no Bible? I was very curious.

It was summertime, and some of the guys and me would gather around smoking and talking, and Father Stephenson would drop by and join the conversation. The first thing I noticed about him was his height. He stood six feet seven inches and had a voice and presence that made him seem like he was nine feet tall. When he talked, you would hang on his every word. He was a very learned man. He had done all of his theological studies in Rome. He spoke six languages and was ordained by Pope John Paul. The spirituality class was his idea. He was a man of vision. He saw the revolving door at the VA, people leaving only to relapse and return to the hospital time after time. Father saw something missing in their lives, and what was missing was God. His Spirituality class was two and half hours long two times a week. The real genius of this man showed in that there were no Bibles used in his class even though the class was held in the VA chapel and was federally funded. Father Stephenson did not allow federal regulations to stop him. He stuck to his vision of introducing us to God. He walked a thin line between church and state.

The day finally came when I would start the class. There was another thing about Father Stephenson that I noticed. He had a striking resemblance to my stepfather. A lot of times in life when we have been hurt by someone, and there is someone or something that reminds us of that person who has hurt us, we unfairly resent that person. I had not dealt with the issue of my stepfather, and I resented anybody that reminded me of him. I knew that in order for me to get the most out of this spirituality class, I would have to first get over this resentment. I called Father Stephenson aside one day and confessed my feelings and the reasons behind them. He looked me in the eye (I did not know what to expect from him) and said in that loud booming voice, "I am not your stepfather." It sounded simple, but it was what I needed to hear. No matter what I was thinking or feeling, Father Stephenson was not my stepfather. From that point on, whenever those feelings and thoughts would come (and they still do), I would say to myself that this man is not my stepfather, and I was able to go on with the class.

I learned many things from this man. I cannot begin to write down all the things he taught me. That would be a book in itself. A lot of what he taught were things I thought I knew, but after hearing him define and sometimes demonstrate the true meaning, I realized I did not know them at all. Through his teaching, he showed me that I could have a personal relationship with Jesus Christ. God used Father Stephenson to not only introduce me to Jesus but actually introduce me to me. I had met many people in my travels, but I never met Ron. I assumed I met me because I am me, but I had never met me. I defined who I was by what had happened to me, by how people treated me, and by my upbringing. But what I learned about myself that I was not, who I thought I was. That was what the world wanted me to believe I was. Then Father Lloyd Stephenson comes along and says, "Ron, meet Ron," and for the first time in my life, I saw myself. Life had beaten up, it had made me hard, but I saw that with the mercy of Jesus Christ, I was not beyond redemption. I could be redeemed. This class had such an effect on me that even after I graduated, I would go back and sit in on the class. Father Stephenson was one of those rare people that if you sat with him for five minutes, you would remember him the rest of your life. God truly did a great work through this man.

Father Stephenson had a heart of compassion for the addicted, and that compassion was not limited to his spirituality class. One day, he was walking the grounds of the VA Hospital when he came upon a group of guys singing. As I have said before, he was a man of great vision. He sat and listened to them singing song after song, and this gave him an idea on how he may be able to help these people even more. Some of the songs being sung were gospel songs, giving Father Stephenson the idea to form a group. This was the birth of the group known today as New Horizon Music Ministry. The group started with twelve guys who wore T-shirt with the group name written across the front using magic markers. Today, sixteen years later, that group has grown from twelve to about thirty. The group is made up of all veterans, men and women, from every branch of the Military and from different walks of life. Some were addicted to alcohol, heroin, cocaine, and reefers. The group boasted black and white men and women singing in unity. The miracle of this group goes on and on with lead singers that were never singers before, others who have never sang before, drummers, pianist, lead guitarist, bass guitarist, and violinist. All this came out of the vision God gave Father Stephenson that summer day in 1992 when he walked up on the group just singing to pass the time. Today, the group does concerts up and down the Eastern Seaboard from Washington, DC, to North Carolina. They do about twenty to twenty-five concerts a year.

Did I mention that I sang with this group? I did not probably because I do not consider myself a singer. I am one of those who "make a joyful noise unto the Lord." I joined the group as a continuation of my spirituality. I saw it as a chance to continue to study with Father Stephenson. Even though this group was his idea, he was joined by a gentleman by the name of Mr. Leroy Jones. Mr. Jones was something of a father figure and a disciplinarian, and he served as comanager of the group. Mr. Jones had many duties from keeping us in line to uniform selection. He was and still is a great source of advice for me. There was also a great lady that helped to form the leadership of the group, and her name is Mrs. Frances Pride. She had the title of the group's business manager who handled the finances and calendar and did a great job. If a church or organization wanted to book the group, Mrs. Pride was the contact person. She was also a great source of inspiration for me. When I think of Mrs. Pride, there is one event that stands out for me. I was working in the hospital when they brought her husband in. He was very ill. They admitted him. I would go by his room at different times during my tour, and no matter when or how many times I stopped by, there sat Mrs. Pride. She was a small lady, and there was a chair in the room, and she would be sitting in it with her legs drawn up under her. She did not leave her husband's side the entire time he was there. I would bring her juice and water and inquire about how she was doing, and she would say fine. She loved her husband very much.

Father Stephenson died before some of his greatest visions were realized. When he took ill, he kind of isolated himself from the group. It was strange because when one of us had a problem, he would be there for us, but he isolated himself when he got sick. He desired to be a source of strength for us and did not want us to see his weakness. I would study the man intently, and there were times I would observe him and see his human side, but when he noticed me looking, he would change. It was like seeing "Clark Kent," and then all of a sudden, you saw Superman.

October 26, 2003, I was ordained a minister of the gospel. Father Stephenson was gravely ill and not expected to live much longer. We would get updates on his condition from the few people allowed to be close to him. I remember praying to God and asking God to allow me to see Father Stephenson one more time before he was called home. I had been trying to reach him, but all my efforts were in vain. Everyone I talked to told me they would get my message to him, but I wanted to deliver my message in person. I wanted to tell him how much he meant to me, and I wanted him to know that I loved him. Since I could not get to him through his people, I turned to God for help. The group was performing at a church, and in the middle of the church, there stood a figure in the shadows. The figure began to walk toward the front, and as this figure moved into the light, we saw it was Father Stephenson. Living up to who he truly was, he knew how to make an entrance. We, the group, were hearing how bad he was doing, and he was the last person we expected to see. Here, he was walking down the aisle. We had thought if we did see him again, it would be in a wheelchair accompanied by a nurse, but here, he was walking down the church aisle as and as proud as he ever did. It was one of those moments where you had to be there to truly appreciate the moment. As he walked, a silence began to fall. The group was singing, but as we recognized who it was coming down that aisle, the singing stopped. The singing did not stop abruptly. It stopped as though someone was turning down the volume slowly until you could not hear it. As Father Stephenson passed a pew, the people stood until he reached the front, and everybody in the church were on their feet and clapping their hands in a standing ovation that I can still hear now five years later. Father Stephenson took his seat in the front pew. He was the only one sitting. The group was crying, and people in the pews joined their tears with ours.

I had prayed and asked God for this opportunity, and he answered my prayer and did it in grand fashion. After what seemed like an eternity, the concert resumed. Clearly, the group's singing took off to an entirely new level. That same hand that turned the volume down as he made his way in now turned the volume up full blast. That was the hand of God. During our concert, we have an intermission, and during this one, I called Mr. Jones aside and told him that I wanted a moment with Father Stephenson before the program was over. And he said okay. I was about two weeks before I was ordained Rev. Ronald L. Warren. With about thirty minutes left in the program, Mr. Jones gave me the opportunity I had prayed and asked God for. He called me out in front of the group and told Father Stephenson about my pending ordination and that I wanted a moment with him. I walked over to where he was sitting. He stood up, and we embraced. And I whispered in his ear how much I loved him, and he told me that he loved me, and then he blessed my ministry. We both began to cry in each other's arms. I did not want to let go of him. I knew I had to let go, but I did not want to. That was the last time I saw Father Stephenson alive. He died five months later on March 11, 2004. His vision still lives. It lives in the New Horizon's who just celebrated their sixteenth anniversary, and it lives in me. In the same God that used Father Stephenson I have committed my life.

Drug War

———⁂———

I am convinced that if we are going to win the war on drugs, we are going to have to fight it ourselves. If we are depending on our government to pass laws or to stop the flow of drugs into our communities, we will lose. There is just too much money being made in the drug industry to think it will ever stop in and of itself. As long as there is demand, and not just demand but great demand for drugs, there will be supply. People are making money on both sides of this coin. There are documented cases where the police have confiscated drugs and became dealers themselves. During the Contra's hearing with Col. Oliver North, we found that the Contra Rebels were given arms, bought for them from the sale of crack cocaine sold on the streets of Los Angeles. The drugs seized in the French connection were stolen from the police department's evidence room by the police and sold back to the very people that the police seized the drugs from in the first place. There was a precinct in Brooklyn that was closed down because the police sold drugs from the police station. There are some countries where the whole economy is based on the amount of drugs sold in the United States, and drugs are their main gross national product.

I believe if they (the government) wanted to really stop drugs, they could. But the order is not to stop drug use control and contain them. There was a scene in *The Godfather* where the Don met with the head of the five families in an effort to reach a peace agreement in order to bring his youngest son, Michael, back home. During the meeting, the distribution of drugs was discussed, and one of the gentlemen stood up and said he gave the order to his people not to sell drugs near any schools and to "Keep the drugs up in Harlem. The Colored people, they are animals anyway, so let them lose their souls." I saw this movie in 1973, and that scene has stayed with me. The order is and always has been containment.

That scene probably had such an effect on me because I lived in Harlem with those "Colored people." In 1973, I had been using the drug heroin for two years. I would love to tell you I did not know what I was doing or that nobody told me, but I cannot. I saw first-hand the devastation of drugs in our community. I saw the bodies of drug addicts, who had overdosed, lying in the alleys and hallways of Harlem. I saw how it took the coroner ten to twelve hours to pick the bodies up because there were so many, and the coroner had trouble keeping up with the bodies. I heard the whispers of the crowd as they took the bodies, "He was a junkie" or "I knew this was going to happen." They talked as if he did not really matter. You are probably thinking that you saw all of this happening, and yet you started using drugs anyhow, stupid, huh. I have to agree it was stupid. You see, I have always seen myself as a smart person, so smart was I that I would show you how to use drugs the right way. But when you get right down to it, the reason I started to use drugs was the same reason everybody else started, low self-esteem.

A lot of books have been written about drug addiction. These books are generally written by people who dedicated their lives to the study of the topic. They have been to class after class and have interviewed addict after addict trying to better understand the addiction. A lot of the authors had been affected personally through a loved one, a relative, or someone very close to them whose life has been ruined by their addiction.

Their opinions are based on the outside looking in. This book is one written from the inside looking out. The subject matter is based on twenty-seven years of uninterrupted drug use by an addict who has been truly blessed to come out of that world and to write about it.

I would like to first and foremost take this opportunity to say that I am not putting down these people who have spent their lives in an effort to shine some light on this disease. It is quite the contrary because this matter can use all the attention it can get if we are going to win this war. So it is my prayer that this book be used simply as another weapon in that arsenal. There is a saying that the therapeutic value of one addict helping another addict is without parallel. Nothing can match it. Even though I have received valuable help from the therapeutic community, the help that I have received from the recovery community is invaluable. At some point, the therapist leaves you, but the recovery community will not leave you. They give you their home phone, cell phone, and an 800 number that is available twenty-four hours a day seven days a week. The people who man these phones are going through what you are going through. They realize that helping you helps them. There is another saying in the recovery community, "We can only keep what we have by giving it away." I now live by this same creed, and I do not believe I am the only one.

I remember one time I was seeking help with my drug problem, so I went to a doctor. He told me that he had a drug that would help me get off drugs. The drug I was offered was methadone, street name meth, which turned out to be more powerful than the drug I was hooked on. I had bought meth on the streets of New York City when I could not get heroin. Just to give you an example on the potency of meth, if you had a bag of the best street heroin and played a basketball game, you would need another bag after the game because the effects of the earlier bag has worn off. Now if you did some meth, you could run a marathon, swim the English Channel, go to bed, and wake up and still be high. Needless to say, there are thousands, maybe millions, of heroin addicts opting to be in the meth program across America. Since it is legal, they do not have to worry about the law, but meth was not designed to keep you out of jail but to kill you. Meth serves the same purpose that heroin did, to kill you. Now because the potency of meth is so much more powerful than heroin, it is my belief that meth will kill you quicker.

We get so caught up in the drugs, and then the drugs have their way with you. Then you look for an easier, softer way out of the mess it has caused. There is a word that makes an addict cringe. Just to think about and saying this word almost bring on the full symptoms of withdrawal instantly. The word is *cold turkey*. No addict wants to hear this phrase. This term to a heroin addict is synonymous with death. We would do anything to keep from facing cold turkey including killing ourselves. We began to think death is easier and softer way out than "cold turkey." But if you want to quit drugs, there is no easy or soft way. There is also a saying in the drug recovery community that goes "You relapse way before you actually pick up the drug." It is in the mind. We think ourselves into a corner where our only way out is drugs. So I have come to believe that if we relapse before we actually pick up, then our recovery actually started way before we actually put down the drug. That means you are still actively getting high when your recovery starts. If relapse starts in the mind, then recovery has to start there too.

You have heard the saying "I am sick and tired of being sick and tired." This is mental recovery when it is true. There comes a point where you begin to do the drugs against your will. When this happens, it is at this point where you have a crunch decision to make, and that choice is whether you are going to continue or will you seek serious help with your serious problem. This is the point I had gotten to before I could receive help. The decision is whether you are going to live or die.

Wind Beneath
My Wings

—⌾⌾⌾—

In writing this book, there have been a lot of people that God has put in my life, and without them being mentioned, it would not be complete. My baby brother was one of these people. I was seven years older than him, and as we grew up, every place I went, he went with me.

I introduced him to sports when he was nine years old. I would take him to the basketball court with me, and he would always carry the ball. He was so small. The ball seemed bigger than him, but he did not care. He was just glad to be with his big brother. While I played, he would stand on the sidelines cheering me on. He was my biggest fan. In between games, I would throw the ball to him and let him shoot a round. Sometimes, when we needed another player because we were short, I would choose him, and because everyone was taller than he was, he developed a nice hook shot. I remember on our way home after winning a game in which he scored how excited he was. He really looked up to me. I would be playing against guys much taller than me, and my baby brother would be on the sidelines cheering me on, telling me, "You can do it, Ron. You can take that guy." I did not think I could, but because he thought I could, I did not want to let him down and found a way to prevail. It was not because of me but because of the faith my brother had in me. I did not know it then, but it was that same faith that he had in me that would help get me off drugs.

During the seventies and eighties when drugs were everywhere, even though I myself became a victim to drugs, I was determined to keep him from falling victim to drugs. We made a deal that as long as he stayed in school, I would support him. I bought his clothes, sneakers, etc. He lived with my mother, and when she moved down south, he came to stay with me and my wife. He began to hang around with some hoodlums and did a little drinking.

My baby brother was growing up. He was turning eighteen, and he had an identity problem. He was known as "my little brother" and was always introduced as "Ronnie's baby brother," never by his name. I believe on some level this bothered him. When he began to hang with these boys, it was his way of coming into his own, establishing his own name, "Tee."

The gang he was running with had a clubhouse in the basement of one of the buildings. One day when he did not come home, I went looking for him. I went to the club, and there were about twenty young boys sitting around, and they knew I was there looking for my brother. One of the guys told me he was in a room in the back. I went back to the room and opened the door, and there he sat with a couple of boys sniffing airplane glue. He had a paper bag around his nose and mouth, and as he inhaled and exhaled, the paper bag would go in and out. He had his eyes closed and did not realize I was there. I did not say anything. I just stood there looking at him. Finally, he opened his eyes and saw me. He was in shock. I told him, "Come on. I want to talk with you." That was all I had to say. He knew to get up and come with me. As we walked, I simply said to him, "If I ever see you putting anything up your nose again except air, I will take your nose off." I do not know if he ever did it again, but I never saw it, and I kept closer tabs on him after that incident.

Being influenced by the boys he was hanging around with, he dropped out of school. Once I found that out, I sat him down and had a talk and told him that he had a choice to make, stay here in New York with me or I would buy him a ticket to Virginia and live with our mother. If he decided to stay with me, he had to go back to school and get himself together. He decided to go south. I bought him a bus ticket, and he left a few days later for Virginia.

I still felt he was in search of his own identity separate from me. After a couple of years in Virginia, I received a letter from him with a picture of him. He was dressed in a police uniform. I was so proud of my baby brother. Even though I knew he wanted to be his own man, to me, he was still my baby brother. I was so proud of him. I showed everybody that picture. I even stopped strangers and said, "Look, this is my baby brother."

My drug usage continued. No matter how hard I tried to stop, I could not. It seemed I was living my life on a treadmill, moving but not going anywhere. I began to periodically think about moving to Virginia. Whenever I would hit a rough patch or lose a job, I would try to talk my wife into relocating in Virginia, but she did not want to leave New York and her family. After about five years, I had hit another rough patch, and my wife came to me and suggested that maybe we should move to Virginia. I started packing my bags right then. I called my mother and told her I wanted to come to Virginia. She said come on that she had three bedrooms, and I could have two. At the time, I had a wife and four daughters. We packed up and in July of 1987 left New York City heading to Virginia in hopes of starting life over.

I personally left New York to get away from drugs, but somewhere in one of my bags I packed was my drug habit, and it went with me. I did not understand at the time that if I was a drug addict in New York, I would be a drug addict in Virginia. I did not know drugs were just as widespread in Virginia as in New York. In less than a month, I was using again just like I had never stopped. Drugs were in the neighborhood where my mother's house was, and it did not take long for me to make connections.

My baby brother knew about my addiction from our time together in New York, and now here in Virginia, he is a part of the police department sworn to uphold the law, and here I am breaking the very laws that he swore to protect. Because of his love for his big brother, it was never ever an issue. Even though he was with the police department, he loved me too much to allow that to come between us. He was voted Top Cop of the Year in 1988, and he asked that I be there, and I said I would not miss it for the world.

On the day of the ceremony, I took off from work to attend. I was working construction and had to return to work after. I showed up at City Hall in my work clothes with dust and dirt everywhere with my hard hat in hand. I took a seat in the very back of the room with the policeman in their dress uniform complete with white gloves and all the city officials on hand to honor my baby brother. I felt so out of place. Not only was I dirty, but I had drugs in my pocket. But I wanted to be there to support my baby brother. When he came up to accept the award, he was given the mike, and he said thanks to all the people that had come to honor him. Then he said there was a special person in the audience that he wanted to single out to say thanks to. He went on to say how this person had been there for him and how much this person meant to him. At that point, I had no idea who he was talking about. Then he said this person promised he would attend, and he did even though he had to come dirty from his job and has to go back to work. He kept his promise. I knew then he was talking about me. Then he said I am going to ask my big brother (I thought he was going to ask me to stand up or raise my hand) to come up. Here I am dirty and sitting in the back row. I have to walk up there before all these well-dressed people. But I was so proud of him that it did not matter. I went up there, and he actually embraced me as he thanked me.

Back in the neighborhood, the dealers and the addicts knew my brother was with the police department, but that did not hinder me or any dealings with me. Yes, there were a lot of advantages in having a brother with the police department. Even though I never asked him, he would tell me the area where the police targeted on a particular night. He would say stay away from this project because it's hot. My baby brother was one of the people I did not have to lie to in order to get money to get high. He would give me the money and then a lecture, which was not so much a lecture as it was encouragement. He would tell me how God has other ideas for me and that drugs were not going to take me out. He never forgot my birthday. He always gave me money for my birthday. I am sure that because he was my brother, that kept a lot of heat off me. Street people (dealers, addicts, and muggers) knew that if they did anything to me, they would have to answer to my brother even though I never said it. I remember going to his house one night for money to get high, and he knew where I was going, and at the time of night, he did not want me out there alone. He actually took me to score in a patrol car. He parked a few blocks away while I went to score. I returned to the car, and he drove me home. It is no doubt he had my back.

My baby brother died in 1999 of AIDS, and I had been clean of drugs for about a year before he died. He would tell me how proud he was of me. He was dying and still telling me how proud he was of me. But I was just as proud of him as he was of me. When he was ten, he would tell me that I could beat guys much taller than me in a basketball game, and because I did not want to disappoint my baby brother, I would go out on the court and win. Now he tells me I can beat this drug habit. I do not want to let my baby brother down. I have been clean eleven years.

A Word from the Author

Coming Clean, I have been writing this book for fourteen years. People would ask me, "What is the title of the book?" I would say I do not know, and I was not being mysterious. I actually did not know. I had a few thoughts about it, but I decided to ask God. It made sense. Since God gave me the book, I was sure he would give me the title. So I just continued to write and wait on him. Then he (God) spoke, "Ron, *Coming Clean*." Like I said, I had some titles in my head, but neither one was *Coming Clean*.

Like so many books before me, I hope someone will read it and know that their life can too be changed. Like me after reading this book, you too can come clean. In order to change, we must find a way to come clean and to tell somebody what God has brought you through, and it is all done to his glory. God blesses us so we can bless others, and as we bless others, God continues to bless us. But first things first, we must come clean with God. We must repent of our transgressions. Since God gave the law, it is him whom we transgress against first. Since we first transgress against God, then it is God whom we stand ashamed and sorry, not man. Seeking man's forgiveness comes later. I believe there is an order to forgiveness. God says let us do things in decency and order. His word also says the steps of a good man is ordered by him. The order of forgiveness is as follows: First, God forgives me for I have sinned against you. Second, I ask myself for my own forgiveness for I had sinned against me. Third, then I ask the world (man) for his forgiveness. God forgives us, the second one asks him to, but forgiving myself took a little longer, but man may not ever forgive you. Sometimes, we have to accept God is forgiveness and your own, but I have found out that is enough.

There are those who will read this book and say "Amen" because they too had to come clean to get clean. Then there will be those who have not come clean and do not think they can. It is the latter group that I came clean for. I am writing and sharing thoughts that I never thought I would tell anyone. Things I swore would go to my grave with me. I write about eating from garbage, being sexually abused, physically abused, being abandoned, having alcoholic parents, and going to jail. You see, God has delivered me from the guilt and shame that I carried for a vast majority of my life. Until God revealed himself to me, guilt and shame were weighing me down, and in "coming clean," I have unloaded that weight.

At the time of writing this book, I have six grandsons and two granddaughters. I also have five daughters. I write this book because I wanted them to know that no matter what they go through, there is a way out. (Jesus says I am the way.) If Grandpa can make it out, then so can I because I have his seed in me. But as I wrote, God spoke and says there is a higher calling. That higher calling is to the world. The world needs to know there is hope in God. God will meet us where we are. The world and some (not all) ministers will give you the impression that God only resides in churches. Some think the more beautiful the church building, the more God is there, and the bigger the church, the more God is there. But God goes where it pleases him to go. God will meet you wherever you are at. You just need to call his name. If you are in a shooting gallery, in a crack house, in a liquor store, at a club, and/or in an adulterous relationship, call out to God, and he will come and show you the way out. I know this because I sat on that urine-stained mattress and contemplated killing myself in a room that smelled of urine when I called out, and God came into that room. He did not hold his nose or frown. He stood there full of compassion for his child, his child who was in deep trouble, and he rescued me. This book is given in evidence of that rescue.

I have come clean with God, I have come clean with myself, and now I come clean with you.

About the Author

As a heroin addict for over twenty-seven years, August 20, 1998, I found myself sitting on a urine-stained mattress contemplating suicide. A gentleman gave me his card a year prior and told me that if I ever get serious about getting off drugs, call him. During that year periodically, I'd look at the card, sometimes even picking up the phone but hung it up. I lost the card. Now as I sat there thinking about ending my life, out of nowhere, God bought the number to me. I dialed it. A man answered, and all I could muster up was "I'm ready." He asked, "Where are you?" I told him, and he came to get me. He took me to a detox center where they refused to admit me. They said because I wasn't a resident of that city, I'd have to pay all fees up front. This gentleman asked how much, wrote a check for my treatment, handed them his card, and then said if he needed anything else to call him. Then he turned and gave me a fifty-dollar bill to get some toiletries. I told him I would pay him back. He said I didn't owe him nothing but that God was gonna raise me up and use me greatly, and when he does give back what was so freely given to you today. Writing this book, *Coming Clean*, is my continuing effort to give back.